SO-CAJ-366

INDIAN COOKING opens with a chapter describing the basic ingredients and methods of serving. This is followed by recipes for sweets, savouries, sour milk preparations, cheese dishes, a great number of excellent vegetable recipes and - of course - curries. Some people avoid curries because they dislike 'hot' food. Mrs. Chowdhary points out that so do many Indian people; the spicing of curries is a matter of taste and if you leave out the chillis you will get a dish which is no less authentic for being mild.

JAICO ⚙ BOOKS
INDIA'S OWN POCKET EDITIONS

SAVITRI CHOWDHARY

Indian Cooking

JAICO PUBLISHING HOUSE
BOMBAY ★ DELHI ★ BANGALORE ★ CALCUTTA
HYDERABAD ★ MADRAS

INDIAN COOKING

Complete and unabridged

Published by arrangement with
Andre Deutsch, London

First Jaico Impression: 1966
Fourth Jaico Impression: 1975
Fifth Jaico Impression: 1978
Sixth Jaico Impression: 1983
Seventh Jaico Impression: 1987
Eighth Jaico Impression: 1990

Published by
Ashwin J Shah
Jaico Publishing House
121 M G Road
Bombay 400 023.

printed by
Prabhat Printers,
A-Z Industrial Estate,
Lower Parel,
Bombay 400 013.

Contents

5

TEA TIME SAVOURIES: *page*

PICKLES AND CHUTNEYS:

Preface

An acquaintance of mine once said to me, 'It's no use making curry for my husband, he doesn't like anything hot.' I think many people here believe that Indian food is always 'hot' This is not true. My father, who relished well cooked dishes, never liked chilli powder or ground peppercorn mixed in his food. It is well to remember that if you only use turmeric, salt, and a little garam-masāla (mixed spices), leaving out the black peppercorns, you can make delicious curries which will be relished even by small children.

INGREDIENTS

Some people hesitate to try Indian cooking because they are not sure whether they can obtain the necessary ingredients in this country. This difficulty can easily be overcome. In London there are three or four well known Indian grocery shops which supply most of the ingredients. But apart from this, I have been surprised to find that I can obtain most of the things I need from my local grocer, chemist or corn merchant. I have given substitutes for some things in the course of the book, so that your Indian cooking can still be delicious, even with ingredients obtained entirely from your local shops.

No curry powder should be added to the recipes. You can leave out the onions and garlic if you so desire. There are plenty of people in India who do not take onions and garlic.

WEIGHTS AND MEASURES

As a rule, the Indian housewife is exceptionally good at guessing the amounts of various ingredients: she uses weights and measures only when an extra large quantity of food has to be prepared. I must point out that it is not easy to give accurate measurements for the water used in some of the recipes. Therefore it is advisable to take most particular notice of the terms 'thick' and 'thin' for batter and syrup; and 'stiff' and 'loose' for pastry and dough. This is even more necessary when halving or doubling the quantity of the recipe. There are no hard and fast rules as to how much flavouring or butter-fat are to be used in the different dishes, so that to make a little variation in the measures I have given in this book will not spoil the food in any way.

COOKING UTENSILS

Most cooking utensils in India are made of tin-plated brass, iron or steel. It is, however, quite possible to cook Indian food in heavy enamel or aluminium saucepans.

Deep, heavy frying pans may be used for cooking dry vegetables, for frying, and for condensing milk.

SERVING THE FOOD

Indian food, including the bread, is usually served hot, although milk curd and its preparations are, of course, served cold.

The modern way of serving the food is to start with one dish of curry (preferably juicy) with the rice pulão.

Then follow the other vegetable and meat dishes, which are eaten with any of the varieties of bread, such as chapātīs, pūrīs or parāthas.

Next comes the sweet, and lastly a bowl of fresh fruit.

The traditional way of serving the food is to have a brass or nickel-plated 'thāli' (a medium-sized round tray) for each person. On it are arranged two or more shiny bowls filled with various foods. Chapātis or other kinds of Indian bread are usually placed in the centre of the thāli. Although most of the townspeople use knives, forks and spoons, yet a great number of Indian folk still eat with their well-washed hands. They sip the juicy food from the shiny bowls, and ingeniously manipulate the rest of the eatables by gathering them up with morsels of bread. The traditional custom, especially in the Punjab, was to start the meal with a sweet dish and this is why I have given the recipes for ordinary sweet dishes at the beginning of the book.

Although basically the same, Indian cooking does vary a little from province to province, and as I belong to the Punjab my recipes will naturally favour the cooking methods used there.

The subject of Indian cooking is as vast as the country itself, and in making this attempt I am conscious that I have merely skimmed lightly over the surface. Nevertheless, I earnestly hope that this small book will be of some help and guidance to those good people who are interested in Indian cooking.

In conclusion, I must acknowledge that much of the credit of this venture of mine goes to my husband, Dr D. S. Chowdhary, who is a connoisseur of Indian cooking.

My sincere thanks are due to my home-help, Miss Florence Rogers, for her cheerful acceptance of the extra work preparing this book has entailed; and to our friend, Mr H. R. Clapp, for his invaluable help in the arranging and preliminary typing.

Pronunciation

'ā' is pronounced as in 'father', 'ē' is almost 'eh', 'ī' is 'ee' (where this is obvious, as at the ends of words, it has not been marked), and 'ū' is very nearly 'oo'. The Indian short 'a' is more difficult: it is the French '*un*' without the nasality. But the English short 'a' is adequate enough. In addition to these vowels there are some troublesome consonants which I have represented as best I can.

Basic Materials

Basic Materials

BUTTER-FAT: Butter-fat, or ghee as it is called in India, is made in the following way.

Place some butter in a saucepan, and simmer for 1 to 1½ hours. Remove from heat and strain through a fine cloth. The ghee thus formed may be stored in glass or earthenware jars and will keep for a long time, with a tendency to crystallise as it is kept. Margarine can also be clarified by the same method and kept the same way.

In my Indian cooking, I use either or a mixture of both, and have found that one heaped tablespoonful of butter-fat, when set, equals 3½ tablespoonfuls (or 1½ ozs.) of liquid butter-fat.

For frying purposes, clarified margarine, cooking fat, dripping, or any edible oil may be used.

MILK-CURD or DAHI. The best way to make dahi in this country is to mix a tablespoonful of yoghurt (obtainable from your local Express dairy) with 1 pint of boiled luke-warm milk, preferably Jersey milk, and keep this mixture in a warm place for 12 to 18 hours. When this mixture is set like junket, the curd is ready.

Dahi can also be made by putting 1 to 2 tablespoonfuls of lemon juice in a pint of boiled luke-warm milk, and letting it set in the usual way. This method, however, does not bring quite satisfactory results at the first setting, because the curd will be rather thin. But, by using 1 to 2 tablespoonfuls of this thin mixture again in a pint of warm milk and letting it set as before, the dahi is greatly improved; and when the process is repeated the next time it should have the right consistency.

In very cold weather, the milk for making dahi should be warmer (not really hot), and the quantity of the curd which you are mixing in should be slightly increased and at the temperature of blood-heat. Some people wrap a piece of blanket round the pot or the jug to give extra warmth. After the dahi is set, it should always be kept in a cool place. In India we make dahi in earthenware pots, but I have found that it retains its flavour fairly well even in china jugs. When using dahi, care should be taken to save a little for making the next lot.

Dahi can be served as it is, while some people prefer it with sugar added. It is readily digested, even by those who are allergic to ordinary milk. Some special cold preparations called raitas are made from it. A traditional cool and refreshing drink called lassi can be made by whisking and diluting the curd and adding a little salt or sugar to it, while in summer some ice may be added as well.

Dahi panir (cottage cheese) may be made by placing the curd in a muslin bag and letting it drip overnight Some people add a little salt to it when it is ready.

MAKING BUTTER FROM DAHI: Dahi is also used for making butter, which is done every day in many Indian households, particularly in the villages. Very early in the morning one hears the sweet, music-like sound of the curd being churned, which is an exercise in itself. Some women say their long prayers (all from memory) or sing their songs as they churn vigorously. Although it is impossible to obtain the original madhani (churns) and the earthenware pots that we use for butter-making in India, I have tried here, and succeeded, in making butter from dahi made with Jersey milk. Here is a recipe which will make 4 oz. of butter. You will need a strong egg-whisk of the Prestige type.

Ingredients: 4 pints of milk, and 3 tablespoonfuls of dahi.

Method: Boil the milk very gently for 1 to 2 hours. Remove from the heat and when lukewarm make it into dahi by adding the 3 tablespoonfuls of dahi to it, and keeping in a warm place for 12–18 hours. When ready, transfer into a large strong receptacle (not too wide), and in summertime cool the dahi slightly before whisking. This should be done vigorously, as gentle whisking does not give satisfactory results. Keep a jug of water at hand, cold or warm according to the time of year; indeed, in summertime, iced water is preferable. Add some of this water to the dahi from time to time as you churn. At first bubbles will form, then they will gradually change colour and thicken. Whilst the butter is forming, continue to add water, whisking in the middle, keeping the butter to the sides. When it is thick enough to gather, do so with both hands and place it in a bowl of cold water. It will very soon become as thick and solid as ordinary butter. All this should not take more than half an hour. Sometimes a second whisking yields a little more butter but usually it comes all at once.

Butter-milk or whey is the proper Indian lassi, which is commonly used for drinking. It may be used in curries instead of dahi, and is very good in soups.

PANĪR (SOFT MILK CHEESE): There are two methods of making this.

(1) Heat one pint of milk in a saucepan, and when boiling add to it ½ teacupful of curd that has been made a day or two previously. Bring to the boil again, and when solid lumps are formed strain through a fine cloth. The whey can be used in soups and gravies. Press the bag containing the panīr with a heavy weight, so as to squeeze out all the whey.

(2) Bring one pint of milk to the boil, stirring a little so

that all the cream does not come to the top. When the milk rises, add one tablespoonful of lemon juice to it; mix well, and as soon as the lumps are formed, strain through a fine cloth and press with a heavy weight, as in the previous method.

Panir is used in making certain sweetmeats, while cubes of panir may be cooked with fresh peas, potatoes or tomatoes.

KHOYA: This may be made by boiling milk fairly quickly in a karhai (a shallow iron pot) or in a thick aluminium frying pan for an hour, stirring continuously when it begins to thicken. When cool, the residue is khoya, which becomes like stiff pastry. It is used in many Indian sweetmeats. One pint of ordinary milk will make just over two ounces of khoya. Full-cream Jersey milk yields a little more khoya than ordinary milk.

KHOYA—MADE WITH FULL-CREAM POWDERED MILK: I have made khoya by mixing two ounces of full-cream powdered milk with $1\frac{1}{2}$ tablespoonfuls of hot water, and working this into the same smoothness as ordinary khoya.

DHANIA (CORIANDERS): This herb is very commonly used in Indian cooking, and it can easily be grown in English kitchen gardens.

MĒTHI (FEENUGREEK): This vegetable is also used as a herb in many Indian dishes, especially after it has been dried. It has a delightful fragrance and flavour. Mēthi, like dhania, can be grown quite successfully in this country.

Parsley, sage, thyme and other English herbs may be used if dhania and mēthi are not available. The quantity of the herbs used in various dishes should depend on individual taste. If dried herbs are used then the quantity should definitely be much reduced.

CARDAMOMS: Cardamoms are one of the ingredients of garam-masāla, and are used in flavouring and to give sweet fragrance to a great many Indian sweetmeats and curried dishes. They are of two kinds—large dark brown, and small pale green. Either type may be used, though the dark brown variety is mainly used for flavouring sweetmeats. Cardamoms are obtainable from Indian grocery stores and from some vegetarian food stores.

GARAM-MASĀLA: The following recipe will make a good jarful of garam-masāla.

Ingredients: 2 oz. black peppercorns, 2 oz. coriander seeds, 1½ oz. caraway seeds (preferably black), ½ oz. cloves, 20 or more large cardamoms, ½ oz. cinnamon.

Method: Sort the peppercorns, coriander seeds (dhania), caraway seeds and cloves, and remove the skin from the cardamoms. Mix together, and grind them fairly finely (not powdery) in a coffee grinder. Mix in the ground cinnamon, and keep the garam-masāla in an air-tight jar. Garam-masāla is used in most Indian curried dishes, giving extra taste and fragrance to the food. Cardamoms can be obtained from Indian grocers, while the rest of the ingredients are purchasable from local chemists and grocers.

Ready-to-use garam-masāla is sold by the Indian grocers, but the fragrance and taste of home-made masāla is well worth the trouble taken.

BESAN: This is the name given to flour made from chana dāl (a split Bengal pulse). It can be bought from the Indian grocers, but I have ground yellow split peas from local shops, and have found that it makes an excellent substitute for besan. I have also ground dāl urhad (a small black bean, split) and red lentils for making mongōrhis and pāparh (puppadums). The coffee grinder used in making garam-masāla will do equally well for this purpose, but should be kept adjusted for finest grinding possible.

PULSES: We use a variety of pulses in India, but the following, which can all be obtained in Great Britain from Indian grocers, are those most commonly used in the Punjab.

Whole Urhad: A very small black bean, which is used just as it is.

Dāl Urhad: The whole urhad, split. It can be used either with its husk or without it, in which case it is white in colour.

Dāl Moong: Very like dāl urhad, but the husk is green. It, too, may be used with or without its husk, and it cooks quickly. I have found English red lentils a good substitute for this.

Kabli Channas: A kind of dried pea, of a pale biscuit colour. There is another kind, dark brown and slightly smaller, which is a good alternative.

Dāl Channa: The small brown channas, split. Similar to the English split pea, which can quite well be substituted for it.

TAMARIND (IMALI): Tamarind pulp, or tamarind in syrup, is not suitable for our purpose, but a definite order to your chemist should enable you to get from him the dry tamarind, i.e., proper fruit with fibre and all; and of course, it can be obtained from the Indian grocers in London. Sometimes it is slightly gritty, and should be rinsed before using.

GINGER: Fresh ginger, when in season, can be got from the Indian grocers, and I have found that root ginger, when well soaked beforehand, has almost the same flavour as fresh ginger. But ground ginger is not suitable for Indian preparations.

Some Indian Grocers in London

Jolly, Lal,
606 Guildford Street, London, WC1   Tel.: TERminus 3049

Bombay Emporium Groceries,
270 Grafton Way, London W.1   Tel.: EUston 4514

A. Abdullah & Sons
2 Helmet Court, London, EC2   Tel.: LONdon Wall 3032

Ordinary Sweet Dishes

Ordinary Sweet Dishes

HALVA SUJI
SEMOLINA HALVA

2½ tablespoonfuls (4 oz.) set butter-fat	2 tablespoonfuls sultanas
	2 tablespoonfuls sliced almonds
4 oz. semolina	1½ teaspoonfuls crushed
6 oz. sugar	cardamom seeds or grated
2 oz. milk	nuts
10 oz. water	A pinch of saffron

FOR 4 PEOPLE. Mix the sugar, saffron, milk and water, and boil for a few minutes; then pour this hot syrup into a jug. Melt the butter-fat in a large saucepan or deep frying pan, mix in the semolina and fry very slowly for about 10 minutes, stirring all the time. When the butter begins to separate from the semolina, and the mixture is a golden colour, it is time to pour in the syrup. Add the well-washed sultanas, and boil quickly until all superfluous liquid has dried off, stirring all the time with a large spoon; this should not take more than 10 to 15 minutes. Pour the halva into a shallow pyrex or china dish, and decorate it with thinly sliced almonds and cardamom seeds or nutmeg.

Instead of all sugar, I have used 4 oz. sugar and 1½ tablespoonfuls golden syrup, and to my mind this improved the flavour.

After it is ready, it can be kept hot in a covered dish in a very low oven for an hour or so. It can be re-heated, which should be done very slowly, so that the halva does not become too stiff.

This halva can be made with wholemeal flour or besan (split pea flour, see page 21) instead of semolina. It is a traditional dish, and a favourite of most Indians. It is considered very nourishing, and goes well with pūrīs—a famous variety of Indian bread. It is usually served hot, although it can be served cold in the summer.

GĀJAR HALVA
CARROT HALVA

2 *pints milk*
¾ *lb. carrots*
1 *teacup* (6½ *oz.*) *sugar*
1 *tablespoonful golden syrup*
2 *tablespoonfuls* (3 *oz.*) *set butter-fat*

2 *dozen or more almond nuts*
1 *teaspoonful crushed cardamom seeds or nutmeg*
1 *tablespoonful sultanas*

FOR 6 PEOPLE. Boil the milk in a large heavy aluminium saucepan. Scrape (not peel), wash and grate the carrots, and put them in with the milk. Cook this on medium heat for just over an hour, stirring frequently with a large spoon to prevent sticking; the mixture by then should be fairly thick. Add sugar, syrup, sultanas and the butter-fat; pour the mixture into a deep aluminium frying pan, and keep boiling gently until the mixture begins to solidify, stirring frequently.

When the halva is of a deep orange colour, and has the desired consistency, it should be taken off the heat, spread on a well-buttered pyrex or china dish and decorated with the peeled and sliced almonds and the crushed cardamom seeds or nutmeg.

This halva can be served hot or cold, and should keep for three to four days. It is not only delicious, but is considered good nourishing food.

KĒLA HALVA
BANANA HALVA

4 *or* 5 *ripe firm bananas*	1½ *tablespoonfuls butter-fat*
5 *oz. sugar*	1 *teaspoonful crushed*
2 *dozen almonds*	*cardamom seeds or grated*
A few drops of vanilla, or	*nutmeg*
other flavouring	1¼ *teacupfuls water*

FOR 3 OR 4 PEOPLE. Heat the butter-fat in a heavy aluminium frying pan. After peeling the bananas, cut them into inch long pieces, place in the fat and fry on medium heat for 5 minutes, stirring frequently. Remove from heat and thoroughly mash the bananas. Add ¼ teacupful of water, and put back on heat again. Cook very gently for 3 or 4 minutes, stirring all the time. Mix the sugar and the remainder of the water together, and pour onto the bananas. Keep boiling fairly quickly for 15 to 20 minutes, stirring frequently to prevent sticking. The mixture should be quite thick by now; add the flavouring, then remove from heat, and pour the halva onto a dish. Decorate with the crushed cardamom seeds or grated nutmeg and the sliced nuts. The appearance of the halva can be improved by adding a little yellow colouring matter before removing from the heat. The superfluous butter-fat can be drained from the halva.

Kēla halva is served warm or cold.

PETHA HALVA
PUMPKIN OR MARROW HALVA

1 lb. of pumpkin or firm, mature marrow (weighed after peeling and extracting the seeds)	½ teacupful milk
	2 to 3 oz. butter-fat
	1 tablespoonful sliced almonds
6 oz. brown sugar	½ teaspoonful crushed cardamom seeds or grated nutmeg
1 tablespoonful sultanas	
1 dessertspoonful desiccated coconut	

Grate the pumpkin or marrow. Pour the milk into a thick aluminium frying pan and bring to the boil. Add the grated pumpkin or marrow and boil quickly for 8 to 10 minutes, stirring and mashing all the time, at the end of which the mixture should be fairly dry. Add the brown sugar, which will make the mixture very 'loose'. Continue boiling quickly for another 7 or 8 minutes, then add the well-washed sultanas, desiccated coconut and the finely sliced almonds: mix well and add the butter-fat. Fry on medium heat for 5 or 7 minutes, when the halva should be perfectly dry and of attractive colour.

Pour onto a buttered dish, and decorate with crushed cardamom seeds or grated nutmeg.

This halva is also a traditional sweet dish, and is very nourishing.

ANDA HALVA
EGG HALVA

4 large eggs	1 tablespoonful desiccated coconut
3 to 4 oz. set butter-fat	1 tablespoonful sliced mixed nuts
1½ tablespoonfuls sultanas	½ to 1 teaspoonful crushed cardamom seeds or grated nutmeg
1 teacupful milk	
5 oz. sugar	

FOR 4 PEOPLE. Beat the eggs for several minutes. Melt the butter-fat in an aluminium saucepan, and put in the egg mixture. Fry very slowly for 4 to 5 minutes, stirring all the time. Mix the milk and sugar together, and boil until the sugar is thoroughly dissolved, then pour this syrup over the simmering egg mixture. Add the well-washed and slightly soaked sultanas, and boil gently for about 10 minutes, stirring frequently. The halva by now should be fairly thick. Pour this on to a shallow dish, decorate with the sliced nuts, desiccated coconut and crushed cardamom seeds or grated nutmeg.

This halva is nourishing and delicious to eat.

SWEET SAVIA
SWEET VERMICELLI

2 *teacupfuls (3½ oz.) slightly broken vermicelli*	1½ *tablespoonfuls (2¼ oz.) set butter-fat*
1 *teaspoonful crushed cardamom seeds or nutmeg*	1 *tablespoonful golden syrup*
½ *teacupful (3 oz.) sugar*	1¼ *teacupfuls (9 oz.) water*

FOR 5 PEOPLE. Mix together sugar, syrup and water, and boil for a few minutes. Put this by you in a jug. Heat the butter-fat, and gently fry the vermicelli in it until it is of a rich golden colour. Pour onto this the previously prepared syrup mixture, and boil quickly for 2 to 3 minutes. Turn the heat low, and gently boil until there is no superfluous moisture left in the vermicelli.

To prevent sticking, it is better to finish off cooking the vermicelli in a moderately hot oven.

When ready, the sweet vermicelli should be a golden brown colour, not mashy or sticking together. Mix in the crushed cardamom seeds or nutmeg after taking the vermicelli out of the oven, and serve piping hot.

MĀLPŪRA

PANCAKE

1 teacupful fine wholemeal and plain flour mixed	1 teaspoonful somph (aniseed), or a few drops lemon essence
3 tablespoonfuls sugar	Just over ½ teacupful of milk and water
2 or 3 tablespoonfuls set butter-fat	½ teaspoonful baking powder

FOR 5 MĀLPŪRAS. Sieve the flour in a mixing bowl, add sugar and baking powder, and gradually add the warmed-up milk and water. The batter for mālpūras should be of medium thickness. Beat for several minutes, add somph or lemon essence, and beat once again. Leave in a warm place for about an hour.

Melt 1 tablespoonful of butter-fat in a frying pan, beat the batter once more, adding a tablespoonful more of water if necessary; then pour two tablespoonfuls of the batter into a teacup, and from the teacup spread it evenly on the smoking fat, taking care to keep the mālpūrā as round as possible. Fry on medium heat, fairly quickly, and in plenty of fat. When light brown on both sides, remove from the pan and place in a shallow dish. Repeat the process until all the mālpūras are fried.

When ready, the edges of the mālpūras will be crisp, but the centre will be more like the usual pancake. They can be piled one on top of the other, and are usually served just warm. They are a great favourite during the rainy season, and in some places are served with rice pudding.

MITHE CHAWAL

SWEET RICE WITH NUTS AND SULTANAS

1 *teacupful best rice*	2 *tablespoonfuls sultanas*
1 *teacupful sugar*	2 *tablespoonfuls finely sliced*
2 *teacupfuls hot water*	*mixed nuts*
1 *tablespoonful set butter-fat*	1 *teaspoonful cardamom seeds*
	or nutmeg

First method

FOR 4 PEOPLE. Sort, wash and soak the rice for at least 10 minutes. Mix sugar and water together, and keep this thin syrup in a jug. Heat the butter-fat in a heavy aluminium saucepan, and fry the well-drained rice in it very gently for a few minutes. Warm the syrup, and add this and the well-washed sultanas, together with the peeled and sliced nuts and the cardamom seeds (whole) or the grated nutmeg. Bring to the boil, then turn heat very low. At this stage it is better to put the saucepan (covered) in the oven for 1 hour 15 minutes, on Regulo 4. When ready, the rice should be well cooked, but not broken or sticking together.

As its quality often varies, some rice may take a little less water in the syrup, and the cooking time may also be slightly varied. Many people mix a teaspoonful of diluted saffron while the rice is cooking, to colour it and give it fragrance.

Second method

The ingredients are the same as in the previous recipe. The difference in the method being that after frying the rice in the butter-fat, you pour hot water on it instead of the syrup. Sultanas are added as before. Bring to the boil and turn the heat very low. After 30 minutes, when rice should be quite tender and dry, add sugar, skinned and sliced nuts, cardamom seeds or nutmeg. Stir with the end of the spoon, and cook very gently (covered) for 25 minutes or a little longer on the gas ring or in the oven.

Sweet rice is very good, and is usually served warm. The flavour of the rice is improved if it can be kept (covered) in a very low oven indeed for some minutes before serving.

KHÏR
SIMILAR TO RICE PUDDING

2½ *pints of milk (preferably Jersey milk)*
½ *teacupful (2½ oz.) rice*
1 *teacupful (7 oz.) sugar*
2 *dozen almonds*

1 *tablespoonful sultana*
1 *teaspoonful crushed cardamom seeds or grated nutmeg*
1 *tablespoonful rosewater*

FOR 5 OR 6 PEOPLE. Pour the milk into a large, thick aluminium saucepan, and bring to the boil. Then add the well-washed rice, mix with a large spoon, and keep boiling on medium heat for an hour, stirring frequently and scraping from sides and the bottom to prevent sticking. Then add sugar, well-washed sultanas, blanched and thinly-sliced almonds, and the crushed cardamom seeds or grated nutmeg. At this stage, the khïr may be put in a moderate oven for about 30 minutes to become brown on the top; but in India, after adding the sugar, sultanas, etc., we keep boiling gently until the right consistency is obtained. This does not take more than 15 minutes. Then the khïr is transferred into a dish, and when slightly cold the rosewater is mixed in it.

Khīr can be served warm or cold. If kept in a refrigerator over-night it is even more delicious.

KHĪR SŪJI
SEMOLINA MILK PUDDING

1½ *pints milk*	1 *tablespoonful set butter-fat*
4 *tablespoonfuls semolina*	1 *teaspoonful separated*
5 *tablespoonfuls sugar*	*cardamom seeds or grated*
2 *tablespoonfuls sultanas*	*nutmeg*

FOR 4 OR 5 PEOPLE. Using a heavy aluminium saucepan, fry the semolina gently in the butter-fat for about 7 minutes, stirring all the time. When the butter-fat separates from the semolina it is ready. Pour the milk on it and stir quickly; add sugar and the well-washed sultanas. Keep stirring until the pudding thickens. Add the cardamom seeds or the nutmeg, cover the pudding and allow to simmer for 15-20 minutes, stirring occasionally. Instead of letting it simmer, the pudding can be transferred into a pyrex dish without the lid, and put in the oven at Regulo 6 for 20-30 minutes to get browned on the top.

This pudding is easily digested, and it is very tasty. It is usually served hot, though some people may prefer it cold.

KHĪR SAVIA
VERMICELLI MILK PUDDING

1 *teacupful (2 oz.) slightly broken vermicelli*	3 *tablespoonfuls sugar*
2½ *teacupfuls milk*	1 *tablespoonful well washed sultanas*
½ *teaspoonful crushed cardamom seeds or nutmeg*	1 *dessertspoonful set butter-fat*

FOR 4 PEOPLE. Heat the butter-fat in a saucepan; add vermicelli and fry very gently until it becomes a golden brown colour, which should not take more than 7 minutes. Pour in the milk, bring to boil and keep boiling on medium heat for 10 minutes. Add sugar and sultanas, and continue boiling (uncovered) for another 15 minutes, stirring frequently. When desired consistency is obtained, it should be taken off the heat and poured into a pyrex or china dish, and decorated with the crushed cardamom seeds or grated nutmeg.

Khīr savia is usually served as an after-dinner sweet, either warm or cold.

PHIRNI
SIMILAR TO BLANCMANGE

2 *pints milk*	1 *to 2 dozen pistachio nuts or*
5 *tablespoonfuls sugar*	*almonds*
2½ *tablespoonfuls cornflour*	1 *teaspoonful crushed*
	cardamom seeds or nutmeg

FOR 4 PEOPLE. Put the milk in a large heavy aluminium saucepan; add the cornflour already mixed in a little milk. Bring to the boil and keep boiling on medium heat for 15 minutes, stirring frequently. Add sugar, and keep boiling for another 15 to 20 minutes. By now, the mixture should be fairly thick— though not as thick as the ordinary blancmange mixture. Mix in half of the sliced nuts, pour the mixture into glass dishes, and decorate with nuts and crushed cardamom seeds or nutmeg.

When stirring, care should be taken not to scrape at the bottom or round the sides too much.

Keep in a cool place, or in the refrigerator.

RABARHI

CONDENSED MILK SWEET

1½ pints fresh milk (prefer-
ably full-cream Jersey
milk)
1½ tablespoonfuls sugar

1 dessertspoonful rosewater
½ tablespoonful separated (not
crushed) cardamom seeds
(optional)

FOR 3 OR 4 PEOPLE. Using a deep heavy frying pan, bring the milk to the boil. Then turn heat low and boil gently, stirring frequently in the centre and keeping the cream and the skin of the milk to the sides. Do this for an hour and a quarter, until only about a quarter of the milk remains. Add sugar and the cardamoms, and boil for a few minutes more. Eventually scrape all the cream and skin from the sides, and mix it all in. Remove from heat, allow to cool, and add the rosewater.

Rabarhi is always served cold. Some people add sliced pistachio nuts to it. It can be eaten as it is, or mixed with fresh fruit salad.

Rice Recipes

Rice Recipes

Rice Recipes

NAMKĪN CHĀWAL
SAVOURY RICE

1 teacupful rice
2 teacupfuls hot water

1 dessertspoonful set butter-
  fat
1 teaspoonful salt

FOR 3 OR 4 PEOPLE. Sort and wash the rice, and let it soak for at
least 15 minutes. Heat the butter-fat in a thick aluminium
saucepan, and put the well-drained rice into it. Add salt, and
let it sizzle for a few minutes, stirring all the time; add the hot
water, and bring quickly to the boil. Cover the saucepan well,
and turn heat very low, then cook for 20 to 30 minutes without
stirring. After the rice comes to the boil, it is better to pour it
into a pyrex dish and cook it in a low-heated oven for 30
minutes. When ready, the rice should be tender and perfectly
dry.

This will go with any curried dish.

KHICHARHI
KEDGEREE MADE WITH RICE AND PULSES

1 teacupful rice
1 teacupful dāl moong or red
  lentils
5 to 6 teacupfuls water

2½ teaspoonfuls salt
1 tablespoonful set butter-fat
1½ teaspoonfuls garam-masāla

FOR 4 OR 5 PEOPLE. Sort, wash and soak the rice for a few minutes. Put the water on to boil in a large, heavy aluminium saucepan. Put in the drained rice, and salt, bring to the boil, and then turn heat very low. Cook for 20 minutes, then add the well-washed and drained pulses. Mix slightly, and keep cooking (covered) on a very low heat for another 15 minutes. By now the rice and pulses should be quite tender, but not broken. If the rice is inclined to stick, put the saucepan (covered) in the oven (Regulo 3-4) to finish off the cooking. If, however, the khicharhi has too much fluid, let it remain on the heat (uncovered) with the heat slightly higher.

When cooked, the khicharhi should have the consistency of thick porridge, but the rice and pulses should not be crushed.

Heat the butter-fat in a small frying pan, add garam-masâla and any other flavouring desired—onions, etc.—and pour this onto the khicharhi. It can be kept hot in a very low oven until the time of serving.

Instead of lentils and dâl moong, whole moong and dâl channa or yellow split peas (see page 22) can be mixed with the rice. The only difference in method is that these are put in with the rice from the beginning, instead of in the middle of the cooking.

This khicharhi is easily digested and is often given to invalids and young children with or without the butter-fat and garam-masâla.

MATAR PULÂO

RICE PULAO WITH PEAS

1½ teacupfuls best rice	1½ teaspoonfuls salt
1½ teacupfuls freshly shelled peas	1 teaspoonful caraway seeds (optional)
1½ tablespoonfuls butter-fat	½ teaspoonful turmeric (optional)
6 cloves	
2 small pieces cinnamon	2¼ teacupfuls hot water

FOR 6 PEOPLE. Sort, wash and soak the rice for a half to one hour. Heat the butter-fat in a heavy aluminium saucepan, and put in the cloves and the pieces of cinnamon, and, if desired, the turmeric and caraway seeds. Keep the heat very low, and fry these only for a minute or two. Then add the washed and drained rice, salt and peas. Mix and fry gently for a few minutes, stirring all the time. Next add the hot water. Mix thoroughly and bring to boil quickly. Then turn the heat very low and cook, either on the gas ring, or better still, in the oven (Regulo 4) for 30 minutes, with the lid on.

This pulāo is very popular and delicious, and goes well with meat or vegetable dishes.

ĀLŪ PULĀO
RICE PULĀO WITH POTATOES

With the obvious modification of using ½ lb. of potatoes, scraped and cut in small pieces, instead of peas, the ingredients and the method for this pulāo are the same as for the previous recipe.

GŌBHI PULĀO
RICE PULĀO WITH CAULIFLOWER

In this pulāo, medium-sized pieces of cauliflower are used instead of potatoes. The rest of the ingredients, and the method, remain the same as before, page 42.

KISHMISH PULĀO
RICE PULĀO WITH SULTANAS

In this, about 4 tablespoonfuls of well-washed sultanas are used instead of vegetables. The rest of the ingredients, and the method, remain the same as before. page 42.

VARHIA PULĀO
RICE PULĀO WITH SPICY LENTIL CAKES

In this pulāo, 5 or 6 medium-sized varhia (see page 112) are used instead of peas. But it is necessary to fry the varhia with other spices before adding the rice. The rest of the ingredients, and the method, remain the same, page 42.

YAKHMI PULĀO
RICE PULĀO WITH CHICKEN OR MEAT

For Meat

6 oz. chicken or meat (cut into quite small pieces)
3 teacupfuls water

1 small onion
1 teaspoonful salt

For Pulāo

1½ teacupfuls (8 oz.) rice
1 tablespoonful set butter-fat
1 tablespoonful milk-curd
1 medium sized onion

½ teacupful water
1 teaspoonful garam-masāla
½ teaspoonful salt
½ teaspoonful turmeric
4 cloves

FOR 5 OR 6 PEOPLE. Using a saucepan, cook the meat gently in the 3 teacupfuls of water, with sliced onion and salt, for one hour, when the meat should be quite tender. Pour the stock into a jug, and keep that and the meat near at hand.

Sort, wash and soak the rice for 15 minutes. Using a heavy aluminium saucepan, fry gently in the butter-fat the sliced onion; add turmeric and ½ teaspoonful salt, cloves and garam-masāla. Mix for a minute or two, then add the milk-curd and the pieces of meat. Fry gently for 7 minutes, then add the

drained rice. Stir and fry for 2 to 3 minutes, then add 2 teacupfuls of the meat stock and ½ teacupful of water. If the stock is
not enough, make it up by adding some more water. Stir and
bring to boil, then turn the heat very low. Cook very gently,
either on the gas ring, or by putting the saucepan (covered)
in the oven on Regulo 4. Yakhmi pulāo is served hot with
other meat or vegetable dishes, and is very tasty eaten with
milk curd.

Some people garnish the pulāo with fried onions and hard-
boiled eggs.

MACCHI PULĀO I

RICE PULĀO WITH FISH

*12 oz. filleted codfish (fresh
 or smoked), or similar fish*
1 medium-sized onion
1½-2 teaspoonfuls salt
1 teaspoonful turmeric
*3 or 4 dried red chillies, or
 ½ teaspoonful chilli powder
 (optional)*

1½ teacupfuls best rice
1½ tablespoonfuls set butter-fat
*2 or 3 small bunches fresh
 dharia (coriander) or parsley*
1-2 teaspoonfuls garam-masāla
1 dessertspoonful lemon juice
2½ teacupfuls hot water

FOR 5 OR 6 PEOPLE. Sort, wash and soak the rice for 15 to 20
minutes. Wash and dry the fish, then cut into pieces of the
desired size. Heat half a tablespoonful of butter-fat in a frying
pan, add turmeric, chopped-up herbs, chillies, garam-masāla,
and ½ teaspoonful of salt if smoked fish is being used, or 1 teaspoonful of salt if fish is fresh. Let this sizzle for 2 or 3 minutes,
then add the lemon juice. Dry the mixture by turning the heat
slightly higher, place the pieces of fish carefully in this sizzling
pan, and fry them on both sides, mixing the fried herbs, etc.,
well into them. When they are cooked, not broken (which

should not take more than 7 minutes), remove from the pan
and place on a plate.

Using a heavy aluminium saucepan, fry the onions gently
in the remaining butter-fat. Add the remainder of the salt, and
the well-washed rice; mix, and fry very slowly for 2 or 3
minutes. Mix in the fried herb mixture and the gravy left in
the frying pan; mix thoroughly, and pour in the 2½ teacupfuls
of hot water. Bring to the boil, and turn hĕat very low; put a
tight lid on, and keep on a low heat or in a low-heated oven for
30 minutes. After that, stir with the end of a wooden spoon,
and place the fish pieces on top. Put the lid on again and keep
on a very low heat for another 10 to 15 minutes. The pulāo will
then be ready to serve.

MACCHI PULAO II
RICE PULĀO WITH PRAWNS

The above dish can be prepared by using shelled and washed
prawns instead of the codfish.

Chicken and Meat Recipes

Chicken and Meat Recipes

CHICKEN CURRY

3 lb. of young chicken
  (in pieces)
1½ tablespoonfuls set
  butter-fat
3 medium-sized onions
4 large tomatoes
4 cloves garlic
1½ teaspoonfuls turmeric

3 teaspoonfuls salt
2 tablespoonfuls stale curd
2 tablespoonfuls broken-up
  fresh dhania or sage
1½ teaspoonfuls garam-masāla
A small piece of ginger. and
1 teaspoonful chilli powder
  (optional)

FOR 8 PEOPLE. Mince onions, garlic and ginger together. Heat
the butter-fat in a large saucepan and fry the onion mixture
therein gently for a few minutes. Add herbs, turmeric, garam-
masāla, salt and the chilli powder. Stir well and allow to sizzle
for a little longer. Add well-washed pieces of chicken and fry
for several minutes. Then cover it with a tight lid and cook
gently for 1½ hours, adding a little hot water if too dry. After
that, add sliced tomatoes and the curd. Stir well, and let the
curry simmer for another 20 minutes. If there is too much
gravy, the lid can be kept off for those last 20 minutes of
cooking.

When ready, the chicken curry can be kept hot, well covered,
in a low oven for an hour or so. It is delicious with rice pulão
and other vegetable dishes.

Some chicken may take a longer time to get tender.

BHUNA CHICKEN

CHICKEN CURRY—DRY

1½ *lb. tender chicken (cut into desired sized pieces)*
3 *cloves of garlic*
3 *or 4 small bunches fresh chopped dhonia, or other fresh herbs*
2 *teaspoonfuls salt*
A small piece of ginger
2 *tablespoonfuls milk-curd*
1 *dessertspoonful lemon juice*

1½ *tablespoonfuls set butter-fat*
1 *medium sized onion*
3 *medium sized tomatoes*
1 *dessertspoonful desiccated coconut*
1 *teaspoonful turmeric*
1-2 *teaspoonfuls garam-masāla*
1 *teaspoonful chilli powder (optional)*

FOR 4 OR 5 PEOPLE. Mince, or pound in a mortar, the onions, garlic, ginger and herbs. Mix in turmeric, salt, garam-masāla and the chilli powder. Using a large heavy saucepan, fry this mixture slowly in the butter-fat for 3 or 4 minutes. Add sliced tomatoes and the curd, and mix well. Dry off the superfluous liquid by turning the heat higher. Lastly add the well-washed pieces of chicken, stir and fry for 5 minutes. Then put a tight lid on, and turn the heat quite low. No liquid is required. Keep on the heat until the chicken is really tender, which should not take more than 2 hours.

Mix well, and dry off any gravy there may be by turning heat higher and leaving saucepan uncovered for a while. Add the desiccated coconut and the lemon juice; let it simmer, uncovered, for another 5 minutes, then the chicken should be ready to serve.

Any kind of poultry can be dry curried by this method.

CHICKEN VINDĀLOO

CHICKEN CURRY WITH CURD AND POTATOES

*2 lb. chicken (cut into small
pieces, with only few bones
left in)*

1 lb. potatoes (fairly small)

2 medium-sized onions

*2 tablespoonfuls broken-up
dhania or other fresh herbs*

*A small piece of ginger, and
½ teaspoonful chilli powder
(optional)*

1½ teaspoonfuls garam-masāla

4 cloves garlic

3 medium-sized tomatoes

*½ teacupful stale milk-curd or
vinegar*

3 teaspoonfuls salt

1½ teaspoonfuls turmeric

1½ to 2 teacupfuls water

FOR 7 PEOPLE. Scrub and boil the potatoes in their jackets (not
too soft). When cool, skin and cut them in halves lengthwise,
and place in a shallow dish. Mince onions, garlic, herbs and
ginger together, mix them with the salt, garam-masāla, chilli
powder and the stale curd or vinegar. Take half of this onion
mixture and mix the potatoes and the well-washed pieces of
chicken with it, and let stand for 1 to 2 hours. Using a large,
heavy aluminium saucepan, fry the remainder of the onion
mixture in the butter-fat. Add turmeric, and soon after put in
the sliced tomatoes, and fry gently for a little while longer.
Add the seasoned pieces of chicken, mix thoroughly and fry
for 5 to 10 minutes. Next add the 1½ teacupfuls of warm water,
bring to boil, then turn the heat low and cook with the lid on
until the chicken is tender, which should not take more than
1½ hours. Add the seasoned potatoes, carefully mixing them
in with the chicken. If necessary, add a little more hot water,
and simmer on the gas ring or in the oven for 30 minutes.

Chicken vindaloo is very tasty with peas pulāo and other
vegetable dishes.

RABBIT CURRY

2 lb. jointed rabbit	2 medium-sized onions
1½ tablespoonfuls set butter-fat	4 cloves garlic
3 medium-sized tomatoes	2 tablespoonfuls fresh broken-up dhania or sage
¼ oz. fresh or root ginger	
2-2½ teaspoonfuls salt	1 teaspoonful turmeric
1½ teaspoonfuls garam-masāla	1 teaspoonful chilli powder (optional)
2 tablespoonfuls milk-curd	
1 dessertspoonful lemon juice	

FOR 4 OR 5 PEOPLE. Soak the rabbit pieces in cold, salted water for 30 minutes or longer. Wash them well and leave to drain. Chop finely or mince the onions, garlic and ginger, and gently fry this mixture in the butter-fat in a large, thick saucepan for 2 or 3 minutes. Add turmeric, garam-masāla, salt, chilli powder and chopped herbs; let these sizzle in the usual way. Add sliced tomatoes, and after frying them a little while, put in the milk-curd. Let the mixture dry up slightly, then add the pieces of rabbit; mix well, and fry uncovered for 5 minutes. After that, cover well and turn heat low.

No liquid is required, because the natural juice from the rabbit will be sufficient to prevent burning, and to supply gravy. If, however, an extra juicy curry is required, then half a teacupful of hot water should be added at this stage.

Cook the curry slowly, well covered, until the rabbit is tender; this will take 1½ to 2 hours. Lemon juice should be added 5 minutes before removing from heat.

Like many other curries, this one can be left in a very low oven until ready to serve, and it can be re-heated.

HARE CURRY can also be made by the above method.

LAMB OR MUTTON CURRY

1 lb. meat	1 large capsicum—sweet pepper—or some fresh herbs
1 tablespoonful set butter-fat	1 teaspoonful turmeric
1 medium-sized onion	2 teaspoonfuls salt
4 cloves garlic	1 teaspoonful garam-masāla
3 medium-sized tomatoes	¼ oz. ginger (fresh or root)
1½ teacupfuls hot water	½ teaspoonful chilli powder (optional)

FOR 4 OR 5 PEOPLE. Slice the meat into pieces of the desired size, removing excessive fat; wash it and keep it ready. Using a saucepan, fry the minced or chopped onions, garlic, ginger and the sweet peppers or herbs in the butter-fat. Add turmeric, garam-masāla, salt and chilli powder; mix well and let it sizzle for a few minutes. Add the pieces of meat, and keep stirring for a little longer. Put the lid on and cook on low heat for 35 minutes, then add sliced tomatoes. Let this fry for 2 to 3 minutes, add hot water, bring to boil and turn the heat low. Cook for another 35 minutes, when the meat should be quite tender. If there is too much gravy, the lid can be taken off for a few minutes and the heat turned higher.

This curry can be kept hot in a very low oven, or re-heated, as desired. It is delicious with rice pulāos.

KHŌRRMA

MEAT COOKED IN CURD—DRY

1 lb. meat (with a little of the
  fat left in)
1½ teaspoonfuls salt
1 medium-sized onion
1 medium-sized capsicum—
  sweet pepper—(optional)
1 tablespoonful fresh dhania
  or other fresh herbs
tecspoonful garam-masāla

½ teacupful curd
1 dessertspoonful set butter-fat
1 teaspoonful turmeric
6 cloves of garlic
2 medium-sized tomatoes
1 dessertspoonful desiccated
  coconut
½ teaspoonful chilli powder,
  and a small piece of ginger
  (optional)

FOR 4 PEOPLE. Wash and cut the meat in pieces of the desired size, soak in curd for 5 minutes, add one teaspoonful of salt, then cook gently, mixed with curd, in a covered saucepan until it is tender and dry. This will take about one hour. Remove from heat.

Mince garlic, ginger, herbs and sweet pepper together, then, using another saucepan, fry this mixture gently with the sliced onions in the butter-fat. Add turmeric, and the remainder of the salt, garam-masāla, chilli powder and the desiccated coconut. Fry for 2 to 3 minutes, then add sliced tomatoes. Let them get tender, then add the already prepared meat. Mix well, and simmer (uncovered) for 10 to 15 minutes.

When ready, khōrrma should be quite dry and of an attractive colour.

MUTTON CURRY WITH POTATOES

1 *lb. fairly lean mutton*
(cut into pieces)
1 *medium-sized onion*
3 *medium-sized tomatoes*
1 *tablespoonful milk-curd*
1 *capsicum—sweet pepper—*
(optional)
1 *heaped teaspoonful turmeric*
2½ *teaspoonfuls salt*
1 *dessertspoonful lemon juice*
½ *teacupful hot water*

½ *lb. small potatoes*
1 *tablespoonful set butter-fat*
2 *cloves of garlic*
2 *tablespoonfuls broken-up*
dhania or other fresh herbs
A small piece of ginger
1-2 *teaspoonfuls garam-masāla*
½ *teaspoonful—or more—of*
chilli powder (optional)

FOR 3 OR 4 PEOPLE. Wash and drain the meat; scrape (not peel)
the potatoes. Fry the chopped or minced onions, garlic, sweet
pepper, ginger, in the butter-fat; add turmeric, herbs, salt,
garam-masāla and the chilli powder, and let this sizzle for
2 or 3 minutes. Add milk-curd and thinly sliced tomatoes;
stir well, and keep on medium heat (uncovered) for 4 to 5
minutes. Add meat pieces, and allow to sizzle for another
5 minutes, then cover with a tight lid. Keep on a low heat for
35 to 40 minutes. Add potatoes, and mix them well in. Pour
in ½ teacupful hot water. Let the curry bubble, then turn heat
low again. Keep it on until meat and potatoes are tender, and
the desired amount of gravy is left. This should not take more
than 30 minutes. Add lemon juice 5 minutes before removing
from the heat. The curry improves if allowed to simmer longer,
and it can be re-heated.

This curry is a meal in itself, and goes well with rice pulāo.
Any other meat can be prepared by the above method.

LIVER CURRY

12 oz. liver
1 tablespoonful set butter-fat
1 medium-sized onion
2 cloves of garlic
4 large tomatoes
1 teaspoonful turmeric
1½ teaspoonfuls salt

2 tablespoonfuls broken-up
  methi or other herbs
1 teaspoonful garam-masāla
½ teaspoonful chilli powder
  (optional)
1 dessertspoonful lemon juice

FOR 3 OR 4 PEOPLE. Wash and cut the liver into cubes of the desired size. Using a saucepan, fry the sliced onions, garlic and the herbs very gently in the butter-fat. Add turmeric, salt and the chilli powder. Let this sizzle for 2 to 3 minutes, then add the liver. Mix and fry for another 5 minutes, then cover and cook very gently for 30 minutes. Add squares of tomatoes and cook for another 20 to 25 minutes. The liver should now be quite tender. Add garam-masāla and lemon juice, and if there is too much gravy, uncover the saucepan and turn gas higher for a few minutes. Otherwise, simmer for 5 minutes and serve while it is hot.

Rice pulāo and vegetable dishes go very well with this curried liver.

COLD COOKED MEAT CURRY

½ lb. cold cooked meat
1 medium-sized onion
3 medium-sized tomatoes
1 dessertspoonful finely
  desiccated coconut
½ teaspoonful garam-masāla
A pinch of chilli powder
¾ tablespoonful set butter-fat

1-2 tablespoonfuls fresh
  chopped methi or any other
  fresh herbs
½ teaspoonful turmeric
1 teaspoonful salt
2 tablespoonfuls milk-curd
1 teaspoonful lemon juice
  (if desired)

No water is required

FOR 3 PEOPLE. Carve the meat into pieces of the desired size, removing excessive fat. Mince, or very finely chop, the onions and herbs, and fry them gently in the butter-fat, as usual. Add turmeric, garam-masāla, salt, chilli powder and the desiccated coconut; mix and fry for another 2 to 3 minutes. Then add the very thinly sliced tomatoes and the milk-curd. Let these simmer for 5 minutes, then add the meat; mix well, and cover with a tight lid. Turn the heat low, and keep it on for 10 to 15 minutes. Add the lemon juice just before taking the curry off the heat.

All kinds of cold meat, including cold chicken or other poultry, can be curried by this method, and the dish is easy to prepare.

KEEMA I

MINCED MEAT AND PEAS

12 oz. *lean meat*	3 *cloves garlic*
1 *teacupful freshly shelled* *peas*	1½ *teaspoonfuls salt*
4 *medium-sized tomatoes*	1 *teaspoonful turmeric*
1 *medium-sized onion*	*A small piece of ginger, and*
1 *tablespoonful broken-up* *dhania, or any other herbs*	½ *teaspoonful chilli powder* *(optional)*
1 *teaspoonful garam-masala*	

FOR 4 PEOPLE. Remove any fat from the meat, wash, dry and mince finely. Mince or chop finely the onion, herbs, garlic and ginger. Using a saucepan, fry the onion mixture gently in the butter-fat; add turmeric, salt and chilli powder, and let this sizzle for a few minutes. Add the sliced tomatoes, mix well, and fry gently for 3 minutes. Add the minced meat, mix well; keep on a low heat for a few minutes, then cover with a tight lid and

cook gently for 30 minutes, stirring occasionally. Add the well-washed peas, mix, and replace lid. Cook for another 20 minutes, add garam-masāla, and cook without a lid until all superfluous liquid is dried up, and the meat is well fried. The skins of the tomatoes can be taken out with a spoon as they rise during the cooking.

When ready, the keema should be a rich golden colour. It should be served hot with parāthas (a variety of bread), and other vegetable curries.

KEEMA II
MINCED MEAT AND BENGAL SPLIT PEAS

In this curry, ½ teacupful of channa dāl (split peas) is used instead of freshly shelled peas. Also, the split peas are put in with the meat, and *not* after the meat has been cooked for 30 minutes. The rest of the ingredients, and the method, are the same as for the previous recipe.

MEAT CHĀPS
MEAT ROLLS IN POTATO PASTRY

For Stuffing

½ lb. lean meat (finely minced)
1 medium-sized onion
¼ oz. broken-up dhania or other fresh herbs
2 medium-sized tomatoes
1 teaspoonful salt
1½ teacupfuls water

1 dessertspoonful set butter-fat
½ teaspoonful turmeric
1 teaspoonful garam-masāla
1 dessertspoonful ground mango or lemon juice
A small piece of ginger, and
½ teaspoonful chilli powder (optional)

For the Pastry, etc.

4 *medium-sized potatoes*   2 *eggs*
½ *teaspoonful salt*   3 *tablespoonfuls breadcrumbs*
1 *pint or more of oil or fat for frying*

FOR 10 OR 12 ROLLS. Using a saucepan, fry the finely chopped onions, ginger and the herbs gently in the butter-fat; add turmeric, salt and chilli powder, and fry gently for 2 to 3 minutes. Add sliced tomatoes and let them get soft. Put in the minced meat and fry for 4 to 5 minutes on medium heat, stirring all the time, then pour on the water. Bring to boil and turn heat very low. Cook for 45 minutes, mix in the garam-masāla and ground mango or lemon juice. When ready, the meat should be tender and perfectly dry; mash it a little with a spoon, and let it cool.

Scrub the potatoes, and put them on to boil in their jackets. Remove them from the heat as soon as they feel tender (not mashy); when quite cold, skin them and crush and knead them for several minutes until they are as smooth as pastry. Beat the eggs and keep them by you; and place the breadcrumbs on a plate. Take a small piece of potato pastry, flatten it on your hand and place some of the meat mixture in the centre; then close it up so that the meat is inside the pastry. When all are fashioned, heat the oil or fat to smoking point in a deep chip pan, dip each roll well in the egg mixture and roll in the breadcrumbs, then fry them two or three at a time in the fat.

When ready, meat rolls should be of golden-brown colour all round. They are delicious eaten with chutney and other Indian dishes.

KOFTAS

MEAT BALLS

1 lb. finely minced meat (lean)
1 medium-sized onion
1 medium-sized sweet
   pepper (optional)
2 tablespoonfuls broken
   dhania or any other fresh
   herbs

some oil or fat for frying
2 teaspoonfuls salt
1 teaspoonful garam-masāla
1 large egg
6 cloves garlic
½ teaspoonful chilli powder
   (optional)

FOR 6 PEOPLE. Mince the onions, sweet peppers, herbs and garlic together, then mix these in the minced meat. Add salt, garam-masāla and chilli powder. Knead this mixture until it is a stiff smooth dough. Divide into walnut-sized balls, dip into the well-beaten egg and fry slowly in the deep, hot fat.

Koftas can be served as they are at tea-time with some fresh mint chutney, or they can be curried in the following way:

1 medium-sized onion
½ lb. tomatoes
1 tablespoonful sei butter-fat
1 tablespoonful stale curd or
   lemon juice
1 teaspoonful salt

1 teaspoonful turmeric
½ teaspoonful garam-masāla
1 teacupful hot water
A little chopped ginger and
   chilli powder (optional)

Using a saucepan, fry the minced or chopped onions and ginger in the butter-fat; add turmeric, salt, garam-masāla and chilli powder. Allow to sizzle for a few minutes, then add sliced tomatoes and the curd. Fry well, then put in the koftas. After stirring for 5 minutes, pour in the hot water. Let the curry simmer for 15 minutes, and then it should be ready to serve with savoury rice and other vegetable dishes.

CHICKEN KOFTAS can be made by the same method. Cold cooked meat can also be used instead of fresh meat.

NARGISI KOFTAS

MEAT BALLS WITH EGGS INSIDE

For Koftas

1 lb. lean meat, finely
    minced
1½ tablespoonfuls besan or
    split-pea flour
½ teaspoonful turmeric
1 tablespoonful milk-curd
7 eggs
Some oil or fat for frying

1 small onion
4 cloves garlic
1 teaspoonful salt
1 teaspoonful garam-masāla
½ teaspoonful chilli powder
    (optional)
1 teacupful water

For Curry

1 medium-sized onion
1 teaspoonful turmeric
½ to 1 teaspoonful garam-
    masāla
½ teacupful milk-curd or
    milk
1 teacupful hot water
2 large tomatoes

A small piece of ginger, and
½ teaspoonful chilli powder
    (optional)
1 tablespoonful (or more) set
    butter-fat
1 to 1½ teaspoonfuls salt
1 medium sized capsicum—
    sweet pepper—or 2 table-
    spoonfuls broken-up dhania
    or other herbs

To prepare meat for Koftas

FOR 6 PEOPLE. Heat the water in a saucepan, and put in the finely minced meat. Add chopped onions and garlic, salt, turmeric, garam-masāla and chilli powder. Bring to the boil, then turn the heat low and cook for 30 minutes; add the split-pea flour, and cook for another 15 minutes. When the meat is very soft and dry, mash and knead as much as possible.

Beat one of the eggs in a bowl, and keep it by you. Mix the tablespoonful of milk-curd and a little of the beaten egg in the meat, and knead once again.

Hard-boil the remaining six eggs, cool and peel them.

To shape the Koftas

Take some of the well-worked meat mixture, flatten it on your hand, and place one of the hard-boiled eggs inside it. Wrap the mixture round the egg, using some more if necessary. Shape the rest of the koftas the same way.

Using a karhāi or deep chip-pan, heat the oil or fat to nearly smoking point. Dip each kofta in the beaten egg, then fry on medium heat until golden brown both sides. Drain well and place in a shallow dish.

To curry the Koftas

Using a large saucepan, fry gently in the butter-fat the minced or chopped onions, ginger, and the sweet peppers or the herbs, for 2 or 3 minutes. Add turmeric, salt, chilli powder and garam-masāla, then put in the sliced tomatoes. Mix and simmer for a little while, then add the milk-curd and the hot water. Boil this gently for 3 to 4 minutes, then add the koftas. Let these simmer for 2 or 3 minutes, then remove from heat. Carefully cut each kofta in half, and pour some gravy on it before serving.

Nargisi koftas are very tasty, and are served hot at lunch or dinner time.

SEEK KABĀBS

MEAT ROASTED ON SKEWERS

10 oz. meat (with a little fat)
1 tablespoonful fine besan or
  split-pea flour
2 tablespoonfuls milk-curd
1 teaspoonful garam-masāla
1½ teaspoonfuls salt
6 small metal meat skewers

1 medium-sized onion
2 tablespoonfuls broken-up
  dhania or other fresh herbs
1 dessertspoonful ground
  mango or lemon juice
A small piece of ginger, and
  ½ teaspoonful chilli powder
  (optional)

FOR 4 PEOPLE. Wash, cut and finely mince the meat. Mince the onion, ginger and herbs, and then mix these with the minced meat, together with the salt, garam-masāla, chilli powder, ground mango and the split-pea flour. Mix and knead for several minutes. It is better to put the mixture on a board and roll it down until it becomes like a smooth dough. Wrap a small portion of the mixture around one of the skewers in a small sausage shape. Paste it generously with the milk-curd. Place as many as convenient on a toasting grid under the hot grill, and keep turning them whilst roasting. When they are well-roasted on all sides, take them off the skewers and serve hot at dinner time, with fresh mint chutney and other curried dishes.

SHĀMI KABĀBS

MEAT RISSOLES

12 oz. finely minced lean
  meat
1 tablespoonful channa dāl or
  split peas
1 teacupful water
1 medium-sized onion
5 flakes of garlic
2 medium-sized tomatoes
1 dessertspoonful ground
  mango or lemon juice

2 fresh green chillies, or a little
  chilli powder, if desired
1 dessertspoonful set butter-fat
¼ oz. fresh dhania or other
  fresh herbs
½ teaspoonful turmeric
1½ teaspoonfuls salt
1 teaspoonful or more of
  garam-masāla
A small piece of ginger

For batter, etc.

2 tablespoonfuls besan or
  split-pea flour
Some oil or fat for frying

2 tablespoonfuls or a little
  more of milk-curd or milk,
  for mixing

FOR 10 KABĀBS. Using a saucepan, fry the minced onion, ginger,
garlic, chillies and the herbs gently in the butter-fat. Add
turmeric and salt, and afterwards add sliced tomatoes. Let this
mixture sizzle for a few minutes, then add the well-washed,
finely minced meat, and the split peas, washed and slightly
soaked. Let these fry gently for 4 to 5 minutes, then add the
warm water. Bring to boil and turn the heat low, and cook for
nearly 45 minutes. Add garam-masāla and the lemon juice.
Mix, mash and dry the meat well. Let it cool, and mash
thoroughly again, and shape into rissoles of the desired size.

Make the batter ready by mixing the split-pea flour with the
milk-curd. Add a pinch of salt and beat until smooth. Heat the
oil or fat (not deep fat) in a frying pan, and fry the kabābs on
medium heat, after coating each one well in the batter.

When ready, the kabābs should be crisp and brown all round. Served at dinner time, they are delicious with chutney, or a piece of lemon which can be squeezed on them to improve the flavour.

Egg and Fish Recipes

Egg and Fish Recipes

EGG CURRY

8 *eggs*	2½ *teaspoonfuls salt*
2 *medium-sized onions*	1 *teaspoonful turmeric*
4 *medium-sized tomatoes*	2 *teaspoonfuls desiccated*
2 *tablespoonfuls milk-curd*	*coconut*
1½ *tablespoonfuls set*	1 *teaspoonful garam-masāla*
butter-fat	½ *teaspoonful chilli powder*
2 *tablespoonfuls broken up*	*(optional)*
dhania or other fresh herbs	

FOR 4 PEOPLE. Boil the eggs for ten minutes, shell, and cut in halves lengthwise. Mince or finely chop the onions and herbs. Heat the butter-fat in a saucepan, and fry the onion mixture slowly. Add turmeric, salt, desiccated coconut, chilli powder and garam-masāla. Mix well and allow to sizzle for two or three minutes. Add sliced tomatoes, stir well, then add the milk-curd. Fry gently, and lastly place the eggs carefully into the saucepan so that the yolks do not separate from the whites. With a spoon, cover the eggs with the gravy from the tomatoes and curd, put the lid on and allow the curry to simmer for ten minutes. Place in a vegetable dish, and serve hot with rice pulāo or any other vegetable dish.

EGG AND MUSHROOM CURRY

6 *new laid eggs*

½ *lb. small white mushrooms*

1 *tablespoonful set butter-fat*

¼ *oz. ginger*

2 *teaspoonfuls salt*

1-2 *teaspoonfuls garam-masāla*

1-2 *tablespoonfuls milk-curd*

3 *medium-sized tomatoes*

1 *medium-sized onion*

2 *tablespoonfuls fresh broken-up dhania, or other herbs*

½ *teaspoonful turmeric*

½ *teaspoonful chilli powder (optional)*

1 *dessertspoonful lemon juice*

FOR 3 OR 4 PEOPLE. Hard-boil the eggs, shell them, and cut them in half, slantwise. Soak and wash the mushrooms well under running water, and drain them. Fry the chopped onion and ginger gently in the butter-fat; add turmeric, chopped herbs, garam-masāla and the chilli powder. Let these sizzle in the usual way, then add sliced tomatoes and milk-curd. Dry off superfluous liquid by turning heat slightly higher. Add the well-washed mushrooms, mix and fry for a little while, then cover the saucepan and cook on medium heat for 15 minutes. After that carefully place the eggs in the curry, and shake the saucepan so that the eggs get well mixed in the gravy. Cook, uncovered, for 15 to 20 minutes (if extra juicy curry is required, the lid should be kept on), shaking the pan frequently. Add lemon juice, mix well, and the curry will be ready to serve. It goes very well with rice pulāo or any of the breads.

EGGS AND PEAS

This curry can be prepared by using 1½ teacupfuls of shelled garden peas, or well rinsed out frozen peas, instead of mushrooms. Otherwise, the rest of the ingredients and the method as for the previous curry.

EGGS AND AUBERGINE CURRY

In this curry, ½ lb. of aubergines (cut into medium-sized pieces) are used instead of mushrooms.

MACHCHI CURRY
FISH CURRY

1 lb. filleted cod or other fleshy filleted fish	2 tablespoonfuls milk-curd or 1 tablespoonful lemon juice
1¼ tablespoonfuls set butter-fat	1 dessertspoonful desiccated coconut
2 medium-sized tomatoes	½ teaspoonful chilli powder (optional)
1 medium-sized onion	
2 tablespoonfuls broken-up dhania or parsley	2 small cloves garlic (optional)
1 teaspoonful turmeric	1½ teaspoonfuls salt
1 teaspoonful garam-masāla	

FOR 4 PEOPLE. Using a saucepan, fry the minced or finely chopped onion, garlic and herbs gently in the butter-fat. Add turmeric, salt, coconut, garam-masāla and the chilli powder. Mix well and allow to sizzle for a few minutes. Add sliced tomatoes and fry gently until they are tender. Crush the tomatoes in the gravy, then add the milk-curd (it should have been kept a day or two) or the lemon juice. Let the mixture cook on a medium gas for 4 to 5 minutes, then put in the well-washed and drained fish, cut into desired pieces (not small), keeping the skin on. Mix very carefully and cover the fish with the gravy. When it starts to boil cover it and let the curry simmer for 7-10 minutes. The fish must not be allowed to become too soft and mashy. If less gravy is required, uncover the fish while it is simmering.

This curry is very tasty with a dish of rice and pea pulão.

PRAWN AND POTATO CURRY

1 pint fresh prawns
½ lb. small new potatoes
3 medium-sized tomatoes
1 teaspoonful salt
1 teaspoonful garam-masāla
1 teaspoonful lemon juice
1 medium-sized onion

1 tablespoonful set butter-fat
3 or 4 bunches of fresh
  chopped dhania or parsley
½ teaspoonful turmeric
½ teaspoonful chilli powder
  (optional)
½ to 1 teacupful hot water

FOR 3 PEOPLE. Shell the prawns and wash them well. Scrape and wash the potatoes. Fry the chopped onions and herbs in the butter-fat; add turmeric, salt, garam-masāla and the chilli powder. Let these sizzle for 2-3 minutes. Add sliced tomatoes, and finally the potatoes; mix and fry for a little while, then add the hot water. Bring to boil and turn heat low, and cook for 15 to 20 minutes.

The potatoes by now should be quite tender, but not broken. Carefully mix in the washed prawns and the lemon juice. Let the curry simmer (covered) for 10 minutes and then it should be ready to serve.

This curry goes well with rice pulāo and bread varieties.

TALI MACHCHI
INDIAN FRIED FISH

14 oz. filleted plaice or
  lemon sole
2 tablespoonfuls besan or
  split-pea flour
2 tablespoonfuls plain flour
½ teacupful warm water
Some oil or fat for frying

2 teaspoonfuls salt
1 teaspoonful garam-masāla
2 tablespoonfuls broken-up
  dhania or chopped parsley
1 dessertspoonful vinegar
½ teaspoonful chilli powder
  (optional)

FOR 5-6 PERSONS. Remove any stray bones from the fillets, cut each one in half, and after washing them place them on a large plate and sprinkle on them 1 teaspoonful of salt, ½ teaspoonful garam-masāla and the vinegar. Mix the besan and the plain flour together, and make into a thick batter by gradually adding the water. Put in the rest of the salt and garam-masāla, the herbs and the chilli powder, and beat for several minutes. Put the oil or fat in a deep frying pan, and when it is smoking hot, put in two or three pieces at a time of the fillets of fish, which have previously been well coated on both sides with the thick batter. The frying should be done fairly quickly to prevent the fish becoming saturated with the fat. When golden-brown on both sides, drain the pieces of fillet and place them on a greaseproof paper before arranging them on a large, shallow dish for serving.

This dish is very tasty with lemon pickle and curried potatoes and tomatoes.

STUFFED FISH ROLLS

1 *lb. filleted plaice or lemon sole*	1 *teaspoonful garam-masāla*
1 *large lemon for juice*	2 *teaspoonfuls salt*
6-7 *tablespoonfuls bread-crumbs*	2-3 *small green chillis or ½ teaspoonful chilli powder*
2 *tablespoonfuls chopped dhania or parsley*	2 *eggs*
	½ *teacupful milk*
2 *small finely chopped onions*	*Some oil or fat for frying*

FOR 5 OR 6 PEOPLE. Remove any stray bones from the fillets, wash and sprinkle a little salt on them.

To prepare the stuffing, mix 4 tablespoonfuls of the bread-crumbs and milk together. Add a little of the lemon juice, the remainder of the salt, garam-masāla, chopped onions, parsley, and chillis. Add a little of the beaten egg and mix thoroughly.

To stuff the fish, place one of the washed and salted fillets on a board, sprinkle some lemon juice on it and place about 2 tablespoonfuls of the stuffing on one half of the fillet, carefully folding the other half on top. Sprinkle a little more lemon juice on it, and coat with beaten egg, sticking the sides together as best you can. Roll it in breadcrumbs and fry in shallow hot fat until it is crisp and golden-brown on both sides. Drain and remove from heat. Stuff and fry the rest of the fillets likewise.

These stuffed fish-rolls are very tasty and go well with tomato and potato curry.

FISH KOFTAS

FISH BALLS

1¼ lb. fresh filleted cod
1 small onion
3-4 small bunches of dhania
  or parsley
1½ teaspoonfuls salt
1 teaspoonful garam-masāla
2 eggs

2 tablespoonfuls bread crumbs
1 tablespoonful ground mango
  (optional)
½ teaspoonful chilli powder
  (optional)
Some oil or fat for frying

FOR 4 PEOPLE. Bring fish to boil, take off immediately, drain, and when cool remove skin and any stray bones. Place in a mixing bowl and mash thoroughly. Add minced onions and herbs (squeezed dry), salt, garam-masāla, chilli-powder and the ground mango. Mix well and shape the mixture into 12 balls. Heat the oil to boiling point and after dipping the koftas in the well beaten eggs and rolling them in the bread crumbs, fry them in deep oil or fat on medium heat. These koftas are usually served hot, with tamarind chutney or any other relish.

NOTE: Ground mango (amchoor) can be obtained from Indian grocers.

STUFFED FISH ROLLS IN POTATO PASTRY

1 *lb. filleted fish*
1 *lb. potatoes*
1½ *teaspoonfuls salt*
1 *teaspoonful garam-masāla*
2 *tablespoonfuls dhania or parsley*
2 *eggs*

2 *tablespoonfuls fine breadcrumbs*
1 *small chopped onion*
1 *dessertspoonful ground mango or lemon juice*
½ *teaspoonful chilli powder (optional)*
Some oil or fat for frying

FOR 12 ROLLS. Wash and steam the fish (not too soft), when cool and well drained, break as small as you can, skinning and boning where necessary. Place in a mixing bowl, and add finely-chopped onion, parsley, 1½ teaspoonfuls salt, garam-masāla and the lemon juice. Mix well, and if it feels too moist, dry it by heating in a frying pan for a few minutes.

Boil the potatoes in their jackets, (ordinary mashed potatoes are not suitable), until they are cooked through, but not over-cooked. Skin them, and mash and knead them hard, using the palms of your hands. Add half teaspoonful of salt. Beat the egg and keep it by you; also the breadcrumbs on a plate.

Flatten out a little of the potato pastry on the palm of your hand, place nearly 2 tablespoonfuls of the fish mixture in the centre, then fold the edges in and fashion into a roll. When all the rolls are ready, dip each one into the beaten egg and then roll in the breadcrumbs.

Fry two or three together in deep fat on a medium heat until they are an appetising golden-brown colour, and serve as soon as ready.

Vegetable Dishes

Vegetable Dishes

PEAS AND POTATOES WITH JUICE

2 teacupfuls shelled peas
¾ lb. potatoes, preferably small
3 tomatoes
2 medium-sized onions
2 tablespoonfuls broken dhania or other fresh herbs
1 to 2 teacupfuls hot water
1 to 1¼ tablespoonfuls set butter-fat

2 to 3 teaspoonfuls salt
1¼ teaspoonfuls garam-masāla
1½ teaspoonfuls turmeric
1 tablespoonful lemon juice
A small piece of fresh ginger, and
1 teaspoonful chilli powder (optional)

FOR 5 OR 6 PEOPLE. Heat the butter-fat in a large saucepan; add minced or chopped onions, herbs, and ginger, and fry gently for four to five minutes. Add turmeric, garam-masāla, salt and chilli powder, mix well and then add sliced tomatoes and potatoes which should be scraped and, if large, cut in halves or quarters. Let this sizzle for ten minutes, stirring frequently. Add peas, and after a few minutes pour in the hot water. Boil quickly at first, and then turn heat low. Cook until the peas and potatoes are tender (not broken) and then add the lemon juice. Simmer for another ten minutes—the skin of the tomatoes usually floats to the top and can be removed with a spoon. If there is too much gravy, it can be dried off by removing the lid and turning the heat high for a while.

Most people like this curry and children simply love it. It can be served with a meat dish and plain savoury rice. Frozen or tinned peas can be used, but should be well rinsed.

SŪKHĒ ĀLŪ

POTATO CURRY—DRY

1 lb. small potatoes
1 medium-sized onion
1 tablespoonful set butter-fat
2 tablespoonfuls broken-up
dhania or any other fresh
herbs

1 teaspoonful garam-masāla
1 teaspoonful turmeric
1 tablespoonful lemon juice
½ teaspoonful chilli powder
(optional)
1½ teaspoonfuls salt

FOR 3 OR 4 PEOPLE. Scrape the potatoes, and if large cut into halves and quarters. Using a saucepan, fry the chopped onion and herbs gently in the butter-fat. Add turmeric, salt and chilli powder. Mix well and then put in the potatoes. Stir for a few minutes, and then turn the heat low. Cook for 30 minutes with a tight lid on. If they are inclined to stick, sprinkle a little hot water over them. It is better to put them (covered) in the oven (Regulo 5) for those 30 minutes. Add garam-masāla and lemon juice about 10 minutes before removing from heat.

New potatoes are particularly tasty when prepared in this way.

ĀLŪ AND VARHIA

POTATOES AND DRIED SPICY LENTIL CAKES

1 lb. potatoes (preferably
small)
3 or 4 varhia (see page 112)
3 medium-sized tomatoes
1 medium-sized onion
Some chopped dhania or other
herbs
1 tablespoonful set butter-fat

1½ teaspoonfuls salt
1 teaspoonful turmeric
½ teaspoonful garam-masāla
1 teacupful hot water
½ teacupful milk-curd, or
1 dessertspoonful lemon juice
½ teaspoonful chilli powder,
and a piece of ginger
(optional)

FOR 4 OR 5 PEOPLE. Using a saucepan, fry the sliced onion, herbs, ginger and varhia (if large, they should be broken into two or more pieces) gently in the butter-fat for a few minutes. The varhia and onion should not be allowed to get too brown. Add turmeric, salt, and the chilli powder, mix and fry for a minute or two, then add the potatoes (cut into halves or quarters). Stir and simmer for a while: add the hot water and bring to the boil then turn heat low and cook for 15 to 20 minutes. The potatoes and varhia should now feel tender, but not broken. Add the sliced tomatoes, garam-masāla and the milk-curd or lemon juice. Let the curry simmer for 10 to 15 minutes.

This curry is delicious with rice pulāo or any meat preparation.

ĀLŪ AND MĒTHI

POTATOES AND FEENUGREEK OR SPINACH

1½ *lb. potatoes (preferably small)*
½ *lb. mēthi or spinach*
1 *tablespoonful set butter-fat*
2 *teaspoonfuls salt*
1 *teaspoonful turmeric*

1 *teaspoonful garam-masāla*
1 *small piece fresh ginger or medium-sized onion*
½ *teaspoonful chilli powder (optional)*

FOR 4 PEOPLE. Fry the finely-sliced ginger or onion slowly in the butter-fat for a few minutes. Add turmeric, salt and chilli powder, and mix well. Add potatoes—which should be scraped (not peeled) and cut into halves and quarters if large—and allow to sizzle for a few minutes. Cover the frying pan and cook gently until the potatoes are slightly tender, which should take about 15 minutes.

Well wash the mēthi or spinach, and cut quite small (tender stalks should also be included), drain and add this to the frying potatoes. Mix well, and cook for another 15 minutes without the lid. When the vegetables are tender and all the superfluous liquid has dried off, mix in the garam-masāla.

Transfer the ālū mēthi into a vegetable dish, cover it well, and keep it in a low-heated oven until ready to serve.

ĀLŪ AND TAMĀTAR

POTATOES AND TOMATOES

1½ lb. potatoes (preferably small and round)	½ oz. fresh dhania or parsley
1¼ tablespoonfuls set butter-fat	2¼ teaspoonfuls salt
	1 teaspoonful turmeric
5 medium-sized tomatoes	1 teaspoonful garam-masāla
2 medium-sized onions	½ teaspoonful chilli powder (optional)
½ oz. fresh ginger (optional)	1 teacupful hot water

FOR 4 OR 5 PEOPLE. Fry the sliced onions and ginger in the butter-fat in the usual way; add the turmeric, garam-masāla, salt, dhania and chilli powder, and mix well. If the potatoes are too large, cut into fair-sized pieces. Put these and the sliced tomatoes in, and allow to sizzle for ten minutes. Add hot water, bring to the boil, cover up and cook gently until the potatoes are tender, but not broken. The skins of the tomatoes may be removed as they float to the top.

Curried potatoes and tomatoes will go well with any other curried dish, meat or otherwise.

ĀLŪ KOFTAS

SAVOURY POTATO BALLS

1 lb. good medium-sized
   potatoes
1 teaspoonful garam-masāla
1 to 2 tablespoonfuls finely
   chopped dhania or other
   herbs

1½ teaspoonfuls salt
½ teaspoonful chilli powder
   (optional)
Some oil or fat for frying

FOR 16 BALLS. Boil the potatoes in their jackets, (ordinary mashed potatoes will not do), and when the skin is just beginning to split, remove them from heat and out of the water. Allow to cool, then skin carefully, and crush and knead until they are like a smooth pastry. Mix salt, garam-masāla and chilli powder and the finely chopped herbs, and knead once again. Beat the egg and keep it by you. Heat the oil or fat in a deep chip pan. Take a little of the potato pastry, shape into a ball, and after quickly coating it with the egg mixture, fry it in the deep, hot fat on medium heat until a golden brown colour all round. Three or four koftas can be fried at a time.

Ālū koftas can be served hot at lunch or tea-time. They are quite tasty eaten cold, particularly with salad.

POTATO CHĀPS

POTATO CUTLETS STUFFED WITH PEAS

4 *medium-sized potatoes*
1½ *to 2 teacupfuls tender peas*
1 *dessertspoonful set butter-fat*
2 *small onions*
1 *to 2 tablespoonfuls chopped dhania or other herbs*
2 *eggs*
1½ *teaspoonfuls salt*
½ *teaspoonful turmeric*

1 *teaspoonful garam-masāla*
About 3 tablespoonfuls bread-crumbs
1 *dessertspoonful lemon juice*
A small piece of ginger, and
½ *teaspoonful chilli powder (optional)*
1 *pint of oil or its equivalent, for frying*

FOR 10 CHĀPS. Boil the potatoes in their jackets; then skin, mash and knead them for several minutes. Add ½ teaspoon of salt to them. The mixture should be as smooth as pastry.

To prepare the stuffing

Using a saucepan, heat the butter-fat and very gently fry in it the chopped onions, ginger and herbs; add turmeric, chilli powder and the rest of the salt. After a minute or two, put in the well washed peas, mix well, and sprinkle a little water over them, cover the saucepan and let them simmer until tender. Mix in the lemon juice and garam-masāla before removing from the heat, which should be when they are well cooked and perfectly dry. Allow to cool slightly.

Beat the eggs, and keep them and the breadcrumbs near at hand.

To shape the Chāps

Break off a piece of the potato pastry, flatten it in your hands, and place about a tablespoonful of the peas mixture in the centre. Fold the edges together, so that you have the peas inside the potato mixture. Shape the chāps into some resemblance to meat chops, taking care not to flatten too much, in case you uncover the peas. When all the chāps are prepared, coat each one thoroughly with the egg mixture, roll in the breadcrumbs, and fry in deep, hot fat on medium heat, until fairly brown on both sides.

Potato chāps are very tasty eaten with tamarind or other chutneys. They are usually served hot at either lunch or teatime.

POTATO AND AUBERGINE CURRY (DRY)

4 *medium-sized aubergines,*   2 *teaspoonfuls salt*
   unpeeled   1½ *teaspoonfuls turmeric*
6 *small potatoes*   1 *teaspoonful garam-masāla*
4 *small onions*   1 *dessertspoonful lemon juice*
2 *medium-sized tomatoes*   *A small piece of ginger, and*
1-1½ *teaspoonfuls set butter-*   1 *teaspoonful chilli powder*
   fat   *(optional)*

FOR 5 OR 6 PEOPLE. Heat the butter-fat in a large deep frying pan, and fry gently the sliced onions and ginger for a few minutes. Add turmeric, garam-masāla, salt and the chilli powder. Mix well and allow to sizzle for a few minutes, then add sliced tomatoes. Fry quickly and dry out all the superfluous juice. Add scraped and washed potatoes. If these are large, cut them into halves or quarters. Mix well, and then add the aubergines (cut into pieces as desired—they must not be too small). If green and tender, the caps of the aubergines can be left on. Mix well and cook the curry on medium heat (uncovered) until the vegetables are tender (not broken), stirring them frequently with a turner or slice to prevent crushing. If however, the aubergines are rather tough, then, during the course of the cooking the curry should be covered for a time. Mix in the lemon juice before removing from heat; and when ready the curry should be quite dry and of an attractive colour.

A dish of lentils or meat curry will go very well with it.

CURRIED PEAS (DRY)

2 teacupfuls fresh peas
1 tablespoon set butter-fat
1-1½ teaspoonfuls salt
1 teaspoonful turmeric
1 teaspoonful garam-masāla
1 medium-sized onion

1½ tablespoonfuls broken-up dhania or other herb
½ oz. ginger (fresh or root)
1 tablespoonful lemon juice
½ teaspoonful chilli powder (optional)

FOR 4 PEOPLE. Using a heavy saucepan, fry the chopped onions, herbs and ginger gently in the butter-fat. Add turmeric, salt and chilli powder, and allow to sizzle for a few minutes. Add the well-washed and drained peas, mix thoroughly and cover the curry with a tight lid. Cook gently until the peas are tender; this should not take more than 20 minutes. About five minutes before removing from the heat, add the garam-masāla and lemon juice. Any superfluous liquid may be dried off by removing the lid and turning the gas higher. Some people add a tiny piece of asafœtida (crushed and fried with the onions) to this curry.

Shelled broad beans can also be curried by the above method.

PEAS AND PANĪR

For Panīr

2 pints milk
2 tablespoonfuls tepid lemon
    juice or

1 teacupful tepid milk-curd

For the Curry, etc.

2 teacupfuls freshly shelled
    peas
4 small tomatoes
1 medium-sized onion
1½ tablespoonfuls set butter-
    fat
1½ teaspoonfuls salt
½ teaspoonful chilli powder
    (optional)

1 teaspoonful turmeric
1 teaspoonful garam-masāla
¼ oz. ginger (fresh or root)
½ oz. dhania or other herb
1 teaspoonful lemon juice
1 teacupful butter milk from
    the panīr
Some oil or fat for frying the
    cubes

To make the panīr (soft milk cheese), add the curd or lemon
juice to two pints of boiling milk, strain through a muslin bag
and press with fairly heavy pressure to drain out all the whey
or butter-milk, which should be kept in a jug. Place the panīr
on a board, and after rolling it out thickly carefully cut into
small cubes. Fry these cubes very gently in shallow fat or oil
until they are of a golden-brown colour.

Using a saucepan, fry gently in the butter-fat chopped
onions, herbs and ginger. Add turmeric, garam-masāla, salt
and chilli powder, and let these sizzle for a few minutes. Add
the well washed peas, mix and cook gently with the lid on for
15 minutes. Then add the sliced tomatoes and the cubes of
panīr, stirring and frying for 3-4 minutes. Next add the whey
from the panīr, bring to boil, then turn the heat quite low and

allow to simmer for 15 to 20 minutes. Add lemon juice 10 minutes before removing from heat.

PEAS AND CARROTS

1½ *teacupfuls freshly shelled peas*
½ *lb. carrots*
6 *spring onions*
2 *tablespoonfuls broken-up dhania or other herbs*
1½ *teaspoonfuls salt*

1 *teaspoonful turmeric*
¾ *teaspoonful garam-masāla*
1 *dessertspoonful set butter-fat*
1 *dessertspoonful lemon juice*
2 *fresh green chillis, or*
½ *teaspoonful chilli powder (optional)*

FOR 3 OR 4 PEOPLE. Using a saucepan, fry the sliced onions and herbs in the butter-fat. Add turmeric, garam-masāla, salt and green chillis or chilli powder. Add the scraped and washed carrots in small pieces; fry gently for a few minutes, then cover saucepan and cook for another 15 minutes, then add the well-washed peas. Mix well, cover, and keep cooking gently until peas and carrots are tender and dry. Add lemon juice a few minutes before removing from the heat; and serve hot with other curried dishes.

PEA PODS CURRIED

The pods from 1 *lb. of young peas*
3 *medium-sized potatoes*
4 *small spring onions, or* 1 *medium-sized onion*
1 *large tomato*
1 *dessertspoonful set butter-fat*

1 *to* 1½ *teaspoonfuls salt*
½ *teaspoonful garam-masāla*
1 *teaspoonful turmeric*
½ *teaspoon chilli powder and*
A small piece of ginger (optional)

FOR 3 PEOPLE. After shelling the peas in the usual manner by popping the pod open lengthwise, divide the opposite side or the empty pod also, so that you may have two 'leaves'. Holding one leaf, stalk upwards, with the inside towards you, bend the stalk end inwards about ½ inch down until it cracks without completely breaking. Then by gently pulling down, you can peel off the inner lining, often in one piece, which can be thrown away. Wash these soft outer 'leaves' of the pods, removing any stringy parts, cut them in halves, quarters, or keep whole, as desired. Scrape, wash and cut the potatoes into medium-sized pieces. Using a frying pan, fry the chopped onions and ginger in the butter-fat in the usual way. Add turmeric, salt and chilli powder; after two or three minutes, put in the cut potatoes and tomatoes, let these sizzle for ten minutes before adding the pea pods.

Add garam-masāla, and after making sure that the curry is well cooked and dry, remove from heat.

Although the preparing of the pea pods takes a little time, it is worthwhile, because the curry is quite tasty.

MUSHROOM CURRY

1 *lb. fresh white mushrooms*
3 *medium-sized tomatoes*
2 *medium-sized onions*
6 *small potatoes*
1 *tablespoonful set butter-fat*
1 *tablespoonful lemon juice*
1 *teaspoonful turmeric*

1 *teaspoonful garam-masāla*
2½ *teaspoonfuls salt*
2 *dessertspoonfuls broken dhania*
   or any other fresh herbs
Small piece of ginger and a
   little chilli powder (optional)

FOR 4 OR 5 PEOPLE. Soak the mushrooms in cold water for 15 minutes, scrape them lightly and if too big, cut into halves and quarters. Wash under running water and drain. Scrape the potatoes, keeping them whole. Heat the butter-fat in a saucepan, add the thinly sliced onions, ginger and herbs, and fry gently for five minutes: then add turmeric, salt and chilli powder. Allow to sizzle for a minute or two, then add mushrooms, potatoes and sliced tomatoes. Mix well, and if the juice is not required, let the mushrooms cook uncovered on medium heat for 30 minutes. Add garam-masāla and lemon juice: simmer for another 10 minutes, and then serve piping hot.

Curried mushrooms are very tasty, retain their flavour, and go very well with a dish of curried lentils or beans.

PEAS AND MUSHROOM CURRY

The cooking method for this curry is exactly the same as for the previous recipe, the only difference being that a teacupful of shelled peas is used instead of the potatoes.

FRENCH OR RUNNER BEAN CURRY

1 lb. fresh young beans	2 teaspoonfuls salt
1 tablespoonful set butter-fat	1 teaspoonful garam-masāla
1 medium-sized onion	1 dessertspoonful lemon juice
2 medium-sized potatoes	½ teaspoonful chilli powder and
2 tomatoes	a little ginger (optional)
1 teaspoonful turmeric	

FOR 4 PEOPLE. Place the butter-fat in a deep frying pan, and in this gently fry the thinly sliced onion and ginger for a few minutes. Add turmeric, salt and chilli powder, let these sizzle for a couple of minutes, then add the sliced tomatoes. Mix well and fry until most of the liquid has gone. Remove the hard

ends of the beans, wash them and cut them into an inch long pieces. Wash and scrape the potatoes and cut into suitable sized pieces, and add both vegetables to the mixture in the frying pan. Mix well and cook with a loose lid on, until beans and potatoes are tender—not broken. Then the lid should be taken off, and the curry should be cooked until superfluous liquid has gone. Add garam-masāla and lemon juice a few minutes before removing from the heat.

Young broad beans (pod and all) can be prepared by the same method.

CURRIED CAULIFLOWER (DRY)

2 *lb. cauliflower*	1½ *tablespoonfuls set butter-fat*
4 *small potatoes*	2 *teaspoonfuls salt*
¼ *oz. ginger, fresh or dried*	1 *teaspoonful garam-masāla*
1 *small onion*	½ *teaspoonful chilli powder*
1½ *teaspoonfuls turmeric*	*(optional)*

FOR 5 PEOPLE. Slice the cauliflower into two-inch-long thin pieces, taking care to keep some of the long stalk with the flower; wash and drain. Scrape and wash the potatoes, and if too large, cut them into medium-sized pieces. In a deep frying pan, fry the sliced ginger and onion in the butter-fat. Add turmeric and then put the slices of cauliflower and the pieces of potato in the pan, and allow to sizzle for 5 to 10 minutes, then add salt and chilli powder. Keep covered on low heat until tender, stirring frequently with a slice—not a spoon—to avoid crushing. Remove the lid and dry off the superfluous liquid. Add garam-masāla five minutes before taking off heat.

This curry is a great favourite with most people, and will go well with any other curried dish, meat or otherwise.

STUFFED CAPSICUMS
SWEET PEPPERS

6 *medium-sized capsicums*
1 *teacupful water*
¼ *oz. root ginger (fresh or dried) or a medium-sized onion*
1 *level teaspoonful garam-masāla*

1 *teacupful dāl urhad or red lentils*
1½ *tablespoonfuls set butter-fat*
2½ *teaspoonfuls salt*
½ *teaspoonful turmeric*
1 *tablespoonful ground mango, or lemon juice*

To make the Stuffing

FOR 6 PEOPLE. Pick and wash the dāl urhad or red lentils, and put them on a low gas with a teacupful of water. Add 1½ teaspoonfuls salt and the turmeric; cover the saucepan with a tight lid, and cook very gently until the lentils are soft and dry, then remove from heat.

Fry the finely chopped ginger or onion in ½ tablespoonful of butter-fat; add the cooked lentils, garam-masāla and the ground mango or lemon juice, mix well, and let it cool down.

Wash and dry the capsicums, and after making a slit in the middle of each one stuff them with the lentil mixture. Heat the rest of the butter-fat in a large frying pan, and put in the stuffed capsicums. Sprinkle the rest of the salt on them and let them sizzle on medium heat for 15 minutes, turning them occasionally. Cover them up for a little while; after that, fry them until they are soft and partially brown.

The capsicums can also be stuffed with potato mixture or minced meat.

How to make Potato Mixture

Boil four medium-sized potatoes in their jackets; when cool, peel and mash them well, and put them in the sizzling onion mixture. Add the same amount of salt, turmeric, garam-masāla and the ground mango or lemon juice as in the lentil mixture.

How to make the Minced Meat Stuffing

Cook ½ lb. of minced meat in a saucepan with a tight lid, using as little water as possible. Add salt and turmeric while it is cooking. The meat is ready to put into the sizzling onion mixture when it is tender and dry. Add garam-masāla and ground mango or lemon juice.

Two tomatoes and a tablespoonful of breadcrumbs can also be mixed in this stuffing.

SĀG

MIXED GREENS PUREE

1 *lb. ready-to-use spinach*
1 *lb. any other fresh greens*
1 *large turnip (not woody inside)*
2 *teaspoonfuls salt*

1 *teacupful water*
1 *tablespoonful set butter-fat*
½ *oz. fresh ginger or medium sized onion*
½ *teaspoonful chilli powder*

FOR 6 PEOPLE. Wash and cut as finely as you can the spinach, greens and the turnip. Heat half a teacupful of water in a large heavy saucepan, and add the mixed greens. Put in salt and chilli powder, and cook (uncovered) for an hour on medium heat. When the superfluous water is dried up, mash the mixture well and remove from heat.

Using a large frying pan, fry in the butter-fat minced or finely chopped onion or ginger for a few minutes, then put in the mashed greens. Mix well and keep stirring and mashing until the greens are smooth and dry.

Greens cooked this way can be warmed up without losing flavour. Instead of mixing the greens, spinach or spring greens alone can be prepared by this method. Sāg is a traditional Indian dish, and is particularly tasty when eaten with makkī kī rotī (see page 120)—bread made with maize flour, and dahi—milk-curd.

SPINACH AND DĀL URHAD OR YELLOW SPLIT PEAS

1½ lb. picked spinach	1 tablespoonful set butter-fat
½ teacupful of dāl urhad or split peas	1 teaspoonful turmeric
	¼ oz. fresh ginger, or 2
1 teacupful water	medium-sized onions
2 teaspoonfuls salt	1 teaspoonful garam-masāla
½ teaspoonful chilli powder (optional)	

FOR 4 PEOPLE. Wash the spinach under running water, and cut as fine as you can. Sort and wash the dāl or split peas and allow to soak for a few minutes. Boil the water in a saucepan, add the well-drained dāl, turmeric and salt, and the chilli powder. Cook for five minutes and then add spinach. Keep on medium heat, stirring frequently, for about half an hour, until the superfluous moisture has gone: then remove from heat. Place the chopped onions and butter-fat in a frying pan and fry gently until golden brown: add the garam-masāla and the previously cooked spinach, mix well, and keep on the moderate heat for a few minutes before serving.

This will go well with any other curried dish.

SĀG SHALGAM

TURNIP PURÉE

2 lb. turnips
½–1 teacupful water
1 tablespoonful set butter-fat
1½ teaspoonfuls salt

½ teaspoonful garam-masāla

1 small piece of ginger (fresh)
or root or a medium-sized
onion
½ teaspoonful chilli powder
(optional)
1 teaspoonful sugar (optional)

FOR 4 OR 5 PEOPLE. Peel the turnips (they should not be 'woody' inside), and cut them into small pieces. Heat half a teacupful of water, and put the turnips in, cooking slowly for 30 minutes. When the turnips are quite soft mash them well, remove from heat, and keep them by you. Fry the finely sliced ginger or onion in a frying pan, add the mashed turnip, and the salt, garam-masāla, chilli powder and sugar. Fry until all the superfluous juice has dried out. In cold weather, this dish, like so many Indian dishes, does not lose its flavour if kept for a few hours and then warmed up.

Parsnips and swedes are also very tasty when cooked by this method. Swedes however need 45 minutes' cooking instead of 30 minutes before mashing.

We use turnips quite a lot in Punjab, and I have found that people, particularly the children, who dislike boiled turnips and swedes, take to this dish very well. Swedes are plentiful and cheap in this country and it is as well to make the most of them.

TURNIP CURRY

2 lb. white turnips (not woody)

1 medium-sized onion

1¼ tablespoonfuls set butter-fat

2 teaspoonfuls salt

1 teaspoonful turmeric

1 teaspoonful garam-masāla

2 tablespoonfuls milk-curd, or 1 dessertspoonful lemon juice

2 tablespoonfuls dhania or other fresh herbs

¼ oz. ginger (fresh or dried)

½ teaspoonful chilli powder (optional)

FOR 4 PEOPLE. Peel and cut the turnips into fairly small thin pieces; wash and drain. Put the butter-fat in a saucepan, and fry therein the finely-sliced onion, ginger and broken-up dhania or herbs. Add turmeric, salt and chilli powder; mix well and allow to sizzle for a few minutes. Then add the curd or lemon juice; let this simmer and dry up. Then put in the pieces of turnips; mix and cook for five minutes. Cover well, and cook on low heat for 30 to 40 minutes, stirring occasionally. If the curry begins to stick, sprinkle a little hot water over it. But sometimes turnips have too much juice in them, which can be dried off by turning the heat higher and keeping the lid off for a few minutes. When the turnips are tender, break (not mash) them with a spoon, and add garam-masāla.

Keep on the heat until the curry is perfectly dry: then serve hot with meat or vegetable dishes.

Swedes are very tasty when prepared by the above method, but they take a little longer to cook.

CURRIED MARROW

1 *medium-sized tender marrow*	1 *teaspoonful garam-masāla*
2 *onions*	1 *teaspoonful turmeric*
2 *large tomatoes*	2 *tablespoonfuls curd*, or
1 *tablespoonful set butter-fat*	1 *tablespoonful lemon juice*
1½ *teaspoonfuls salt*	½ *teaspoonful chilli powder (optional)*

FOR 3 OR 4 PEOPLE. Scrape the marrow, and cut into small pieces (not too small); unless the seeds are very hard they can be left in. Wash well and let the pieces drain. Using a saucepan, fry in the butter-fat on a low heat the onions cut into large pieces, and let them sizzle for a minute or two. Add the turmeric, salt, garam-masāla and chilli powder. Mix well, add sliced tomatoes and fry them for a few minutes; then add the curd or lemon juice. Mix and cook this mixture until superfluous liquid is dried off; add the pieces of marrow. Mix in well, and cook uncovered for 5 minutes. Then put lid on, and cook for another 15 to 20 minutes: uncover and let the superfluous liquid dry off.

Marrow should be well cooked and dry before removing from the heat.

CURRIED LEEKS

8 *medium-sized leeks*	1 *teaspoonful turmeric*
4 *varhia (spicy dried lentil cakes—see page 112)*	½ *teaspoonful garam-masāla*
1 *tablespoonful set butter-fat*	½ *teaspoonful chilli powder (optional)*
3 *medium-sized tomatoes*	2 *small pieces ginger*
1 *teaspoonful salt*	½ *teacupful hot water*
2 *tablespoonfuls milk-curd or*	
1 *dessertspoonful lemon juice*	

FOR 4 PEOPLE. Remove the rough heads and most of the green
tails from the leeks, and make two or three cuts lengthwise in
each one, taking care not to cut them through completely; wash
them under running water and allow to drain.

Using a saucepan, fry the varhia (whole or broken in two
or three pieces each) slowly in the butter-fat for 2-3 minutes.
Add curmeric, salt, garam-masāla, chilli powder and the
chopped ginger. Mix well and let it sizzle for a minute or two.
Then add the leeks, frying gently without a lid for a little
while, and stirring occasionally, then pour in the hot water.
Bring to the boil, turn the heat quite low, cover and cook
gently for the next 20 minutes. Next add the sliced tomatoes,
milk-curd or lemon juice. Mix thoroughly, taking care not to
crush the leeks. Simmer for 15 to 20 minutes.

STUFFED AUBERGINES

8 *fairly small aubergines*
2 *medium-sized onions*
1 *small capsicum (sweet*
  pepper)
    tablespoonful set butter-fat
1 *teaspoonful turmeric*
2 *teaspoonfuls salt*

1 *teaspoonful garam-masāla*
1 *tablespoonful ground mango*
  or lemon juice
1 *small piece of ginger and*
  ½ teaspoonful chilli powder
  (optional)

FOR 4 PEOPLE. Mince onions, capsicums and ginger together
Put a teaspoonful of butter-fat in a small frying pan, and
slowly fry the onion mixture. Add the turmeric, 1½ teaspoonfuls
of salt, garam-masāla, chilli powder and the ground mango or
lemon juice. Fry this mixture well, so that no moisture is left
in it, then remove from heat.

Wash and dry the aubergines, and make two deep cuts in
each, keeping the tops and bottoms smooth. Stuff as much as

possible of the fried onion mixture into these cuts, then loosely
tie some clean cotton round each aubergine. Heat the rest of
the butter-fat in a large, deep frying pan, and put the aubergines in. Sprinkle the remaining ½ teaspoonful of salt over
them, and fry gently, turning them with a slice every now and
then. Cover them with an enamel plate for part of the time,
so that they become tender. When well cooked (but not
broken) and dry, remove from heat and serve hot.

BHARTHA

AUBERGINE PURÉE

2 *large aubergines*
½ *lb. tomatoes*
2 *medium-sized onions*
1½ *tablespoonfuls set butter-fat*
1 *piece of ginger and*
  ½ *teaspoonful chilli powder*
  (optional)

½ *teaspoonful turmeric*
2 *teaspoonfuls salt*
1 *teaspoonful garam-masāla*
2 *tablespoonfuls freshly broken-up dhania or any other fresh herbs*

FOR 4 PEOPLE. Place the aubergines under a grill or toaster, or
over the gas ring, turn frequently, holding them by their tops.
The skin will gradually get black and the aubergines will
become soft inside. They should be soft from top to bottom.
Place under running water and carefully peel by hand. Drain
the water out of them and mash well. Put the butter-fat into
a frying-pan on a low heat; cut the onions and ginger into small
pieces and fry them slowly until they are a light brown colour,
then add turmeric, salt, garam-masāla and chilli powder. Mix
well, then add tomatoes cut into small pieces. Let the mixture
dry up while frying, and lastly add the aubergines. Fry the

whole mixture for five to ten minutes, stirring continuously. When the mixture is fairly solid, it is ready.

Bhartha should be served hot, and will go with any juicy vegetable or meat dishes.

BAND GOBHI
CURRIED CABBAGE

1½ lb. firm, whitish cabbage	A small piece of ginger, root or
1 tablespoonful set butter-fat	fresh, or 1 medium-sized
2 teaspoonfuls salt	onion
1 teaspoonful turmeric	½ teaspoonful chilli powder
1 teaspoonful garam-masāla	(optional)

FOR 4 PEOPLE. Shred the cabbage (not too small) and after washing well, allow to drain. Using a large, heavy frying pan, fry in the butter-fat the finely sliced ginger or onion. After a few minutes, add turmeric, salt and chilli powder; mix well, and then put in the cabbage. To start with, fill the frying pan to capacity, as during the cooking the cabbage will naturally shrink. Stir with a slice (not a spoon) to prevent crushing. Cook without lid on medium heat for 15 minutes; then, when the superfluous liquid begins to dry off, cover the frying pan with a lid or enamel plate. Continue to cook gently until cabbage is tender, then uncover again. Fry quickly until the curry is quite dry, then add garam-masāla and mix well. When ready, the curried cabbage should be perfectly dry, but not mashy.

Brussels sprouts can be curried by the above method, but they should be kept whole, not shredded.

BANANA CURRY

1½ lbs. bananas (slightly under-ripe)
1 dessertspoonful set butter-fat
1 teaspoonful salt
½ teaspoonful turmeric
½ teaspoonful caraway seeds (optional)

½ teaspoonful garam-masāla
½ teaspoonful chilli powder (optional)
2 tablespoonfuls dahi or
  1 tablespoonful milk and
  1 tablespoonful lemon juice

FOR 3 PEOPLE. After peeling the bananas cut them into lengths about 1 inch long. Using a thick frying pan, heat the butter-fat, add the turmeric and caraway seeds. After a few minutes put in the pieces of banana, add the salt and chilli powder, mix and cook gently (uncovered) for 5-7 minutes. Add the garam-masāla and the milk-curd. Stir with the end of a spoon, taking care not to crush the bananas. Simmer for about another seven minutes, until all the superfluous juice is dried up and the bananas are tender but not broken: the curry will then be ready.

It should be served hot with curried meat or vegetable dishes.

Dried Beans, Peas, Lentils, Varhia & Pāparh
(Puppadums)

Dried Beans, Peas, Lentils, Varhia & Pāparh (Puppadums)

DĀL URHAD (DRY)

SPLIT BLACK BEANS

1½ teacupfuls dāl urhad
  (see page 22)
1½ teacupfuls hot water
½ lb. tomatoes
2 medium-sized onions
1 tablespoonful set butter-fat
2½ teaspoonfuls salt

1 teaspoonful turmeric
½ oz. broken-up mēthi, or any
  other fresh herbs
1 teaspoonful garam-masāla
A little chopped ginger and
  chilli powder (optional)

FOR 5 OR 6 PEOPLE. Sort and wash the dāl and allow to soak for a little while. Using a thick saucepan, fry gently in the butter-fat the thinly sliced onions, ginger and the herbs for a few minutes. Care must be taken not to let these get really brown. Add turmeric, salt and chilli powder, mix well, and add sliced tomatoes. Let the mixture sizzle for a few minutes, and then put in the washed and drained beans. Keep stirring for another five minutes, then pour in the hot water. Bring quickly to the boil, and after that you can either cook them (well covered) on a very low heat for 30-40 minutes, or better still, they can be placed (well covered) in the oven (Regulo 4) for the same length of time. The garam-masāla can be mixed in the beans a few minutes before removing from the heat.

This dāl is served hot, and the flavour is improved by squeezing a little lemon juice on it.

WHOLE URHAD
WHOLE BLACK BEANS

1½ *teacupfuls urhad
(see page 22)*
4½ *teacupfuls water*
1 *teaspoonful turmeric*
2 *tablespoonfuls fresh chopped dhania or other fresh herbs*
1 *tablespoonful set butter-fat*

1½ *teaspoonfuls garam-masāla*
¼ *oz. fresh or dried ginger, or 2 medium-sized onions*
½ *teaspoonful chilli powder (optional)*
1½ *teaspoonfuls salt*

FOR 5 OR 6 PEOPLE. Sort and wash the whole urhad, boil the water in a saucepan, and put them in. Add salt and turmeric, and cook on a low heat for an hour and a half.

Using a small frying pan, fry the ginger or onions in the butter-fat, add garam-masāla, chilli powder and chopped dhania or other herbs. Allow to sizzle for a few minutes, and then add this to the urhad in the saucepan. Mix well, and keep on a low heat for ten minutes longer.

This dāl is eaten with chapātīs or rice, and is considered to be very nourishing.

DĀL CHANNA
SPLIT PEAS

1 *teacupful dāl channa
(see page 22)*
3 *teacupfuls water*
1 *tablespoonful set butter-fat*
1½ *teaspoonfuls salt*
1 *teaspoonful turmeric*
1 *teaspoonful garam-masāla*

1 *medium-sized onion*
2 *tablespoonfuls broken-up mēthi, or other fresh herbs*
A piece of ginger and ½ teaspoonful chilli powder (optional)

FOR 4 PEOPLE. Sort and wash the dāl, and let it soak for 30 minutes or so. Boil the water in a saucepan, and after draining the dāl, add that to it, together with salt, turmeric, and chilli powder. Bring to the boil, then turn heat quite low, and keeping the lid on cook until the dāl is tender, which will take about an hour. Mix well with a spoon, without allowing the dāl to get 'mashy'.

Place the butter-fat in the frying pan, and fry the chopped onions and ginger; add herbs and garam-masāla just before taking off. Pour this mixture on to the dāl, which should now be ready for serving.

Dāl urhad and the yellow split peas which we get in the shops here can be prepared by using the same ingredients and method. Some people mix dāl channa and urhad together, which makes the dish even tastier.

DĀL MOONG

SPLIT GREEN BEANS OR RED LENTILS

1 *teacupful dāl moong (see page 22)*	2 *tablespoonfuls broken dhania, or any other fresh herbs*
2½ *teacupfuls water*	1½ *teaspoonfuls salt*
1 *dessertspoonful set butter-fat*	1 *teaspoonful turmeric*
1 *medium-sized onion*	½ *teaspoonful chilli powder (optional)*
1 *teaspoonful garam-masāla*	

FOR 4 PEOPLE. The cooking method for this dāl is exactly the same as for dāl channa (see above), but the cooking time is reduced to just over fifteen minutes, instead of one hour. This dāl should also be served well garnished with fried onions, herbs and garam-masāla.

This dish is considered to be very easily digested, and is often given (without the onion mixture and the chilli powder) to very young children, invalids and convalescents.

Red lentils which we get in the shops here can be prepared by the above method and with the same ingredients.

KABLI CHANNAS
WHOLE BENGAL DRIED PEAS

1½ teacupfuls (8½ oz.) channas (see page 22)

1½ tablespoonfuls set butter-fat

¼ lb. tomatoes

1½ oz. tamarinds (or 3 table-spoons of lemon juice)

2 teaspoonfuls salt

1 teaspoonful turmeric

2 medium-sized onions

4 small cloves of garlic

2 tablespoonfuls broken-up dhania or any other fresh herbs

1½ teaspoonfuls garam-masóla

¼ oz. chopped ginger

2 fresh green chillies, or ½ teaspoonful of chilli powder (optional)

FOR 5 OR 6 PEOPLE. Sort, wash and soak the channas in ample water for at least 12 hours. Then you can either boil them in the same water on medium heat until they are very soft (almost splitting), or in the pressure cooker for 30 minutes, using a little less water than shown on the cooker chart.

Pour the stock from the channas into a jug. Mince the onions, garlic, ginger, chillies and herbs together, mix in the turmeric, salt, chilli powder and garam-masála. Heat the butter-fat in a saucepan, and gently fry the mixture. Add thinly sliced tomatoes, and allow to sizzle for seven minutes. Add the channas, mix well, and keep on medium heat a little longer. Add ½ teacupful of the stock, and when gently boiling add tamarindus juice, which is prepared as follows.

Rinse the tamarinds and pour on them 1¼ teacupfuls of stock from the jug (hot water instead of stock if necessary). Soak the fruit well and remove all pulp; strain through a sieve (not too fine), and add to the channas. If tamarind is not available, lemon juice could be used. Let the curry simmer on the gas ring or in the oven for 20 to 30 minutes. Channas are tastier if prepared a few hours in advance, then heated through and served piping hot. They are delicious with savoury rice, and with various dry vegetable or meat dishes. Some people improve the flavour still more by cooking a few pieces of lamb or mutton with the channas.

Tamarind, of course, one can get from the chemist, but channas have to be obtained from an Indian grocer, and I am afraid there is no real substitute for them in ordinary shops.

HARICOT AND OTHER DRIED BEANS

1 *teacupful dried beans*
1 *tablespoonful set butter-fat*
1 *medium-sized onion*
2 *flakes of garlic*
1 *teaspoonful garam-masāla*
¼ *oz. ginger, fresh or root, and*
   ½ *teaspoonful chilli powder*
   —*if desired*
2 *medium-sized tomatoes*

1 *medium-sized sweet pepper;*
   some fresh herbs
1½ *to 2 teaspoonfuls salt*
1 *teaspoonful turmeric*
2 *oz. tamarinds, or 1 table-*
   spoonful lemon juice
A few pieces of meat or marrow
   bones—if desired

FOR 4 TO 5 PEOPLE. Sort, wash and soak the beans for 8 hours; then rinse, and put them on to boil, with a teaspoonful of salt and 4 teacupfuls of water and the meat or bones, on a low heat, stirring occasionally. Boil until quite tender, which will take about 1¼ hours, then remove from heat.

Using another saucepan, fry in the butter-fat the chopped onions, herbs, ginger and garlic; add turmeric, 1 teaspoonful salt, garam-masāla and the chilli powder. Let this sizzle for a few minutes, then add the sliced tomatoes, let them mix and get tender. Next add the beans and meat without the stock, mix and fry gently for five minutes; then add the stock. Rinse and soak the tamarinds in a teacupful of water (hot) for 2 or 3 minutes, then rub the fruit with the fingers so that all the pulp comes off the stones. Pour this pulp and juice of the tamarinds on the simmering beans. If tamarind is not available, then lemon juice can be used.

The cooking time will vary with different kinds of dried beans.

Curried beans are very tasty served with rice pulāo or other vegetable dishes, and should be served hot.

MONGŌRHIS I

RISSOLES MADE WITH DĀL OR LENTILS

1 *teacupful dāl moong, urhad* (*see page* 22), *or red lentils*	1 *teaspoonful caraway seeds*
1 *teaspoonful salt*	½ *teaspoonful chilli powder* (*optional*)
½ *teaspoonful turmeric*	*Some oil or fat for frying*
½ *teaspoonful garam-masāla*	

FOR 18 OR 20 MONGŌRHIS. Sort, wash and soak the dāl for 18 to 24 hours. After that, drain it well, and putting a portion of it in a large mortar, crush it as much as possible with the pestle. When all the dāl has been thus treated, put it in a mixing bowl, add the other ingredients, and beat the mixture for several minutes. Heat the oil or fat to smoking point, and taking some of the mixture, either by hand or in a spoon, drop it in the smoking fat. Fry 5 or 6 mongōrhis at a time on medium heat.

These mongōrhis can also be served hot or cold at tea-time, or they can be curried by the same method and using the same ingredients as in the following recipe.

MONGŌRHIS II

RISSOLES MADE WITH DĀL OR LENTILS

1 teacupful dāl moong, urhad
  (see page 22) or red lentils
1½ teacupfuls warm water
1½ teaspoonfuls salt
1 teaspoonful caraway seeds

½ teaspoonful chilli powder
  (optional)
½ teaspoonful garam-masāla
Some oil or fat for frying

FOR 24 SMALL MONGŌRHIS. Sort the dāl and rub it with a clean cloth; grind in a coffee mill, and pass the flour through a sieve. The roughage can be used in soups, and you should have ¾ of a teacupful of flour. Gradually add the warm water, and make a thick batter. Beat with a spoon for several minutes, then add salt, garam-masāla and the caraway seeds. Let stand for one hour, then beat thoroughly again. Heat the oil or fat in a deep frying pan or chip pan on a medium heat; when smoking hot, drop in small portions of the lentil mixture with a spoon or your clean hands. Fry four or five mongōrhis at a time on medium heat. When golden brown all round, take out of pan, drain well and place on a large shallow dish. Monghōris can be served as they are, hot or cold, at tea-time, or they can be curried by the following method:

For the curry

1 tablespoonful butter-fat
1 medium-sized onion
1 medium-sized sweet
  pepper, or 1 tablespoonful
  fresh chopped herbs
4 large tomatoes
1 teaspoonful salt

1 teaspoonful garam-masāla
½ teaspoonful chilli powder
1 teacupful hot water
½ teacupful milk-curd, or
  1 tablespoonful lemon juice
1 teaspoonful turmeric

Chop and fry the onion and sweet pepper in the butter-fat in a heavy saucepan; add turmeric, salt, garam-masāla and chilli powder, mix well, and then add the sliced tomatoes. Let the mixture sizzle for a few minutes, and then add the mongōrhis. Stir well, and leave on a low heat for a little while longer. Add hot water and the curd, bring to the boil, and after covering it, allow to simmer for 10 to 15 minutes.

This curry is very tasty and goes well with rice pulāo.

VARHIA

SMALL DRIED SPICY LENTIL CAKES

1 teacupful *dāl urhad* (see page 22) *or ordinary red lentils*

2 tablespoonfuls *dāl urhad or lentil flour*

1 teaspoonful *caraway seeds*

1½ teaspoonfuls *garam-masāla*

1 tablespoonful *coriander seeds*

2 teaspoonfuls *salt*

½ teaspoonful *turmeric*

1 teaspoonful *chilli powder* (*optional*)

A small lump (*about the size of a haricot bean*) *of asafœtida* (*optional*)

FOR 18 VARHIA. Sort and wash the dāl or lentils, and soak for 18 to 24 hours; then drain them, and putting a portion at a time in a large mortar, crush them with the pestle as much as you can. When completed, put all into a mixing bowl, add the flour (made by grinding the lentils in a coffee mill), and the rest of the ingredients. The asafœtida should be crushed before mixing. Beat and knead the mixture for several minutes, then leave it in a warm place for 2 to 4 hours. Then knead it once again, and shape the varhia by getting some of the mixture in your hand and letting it drop onto a well-greased plate. Continue the process until all the mixture is used up. Place the varhia in the sun to dry, or if there is no possibility of drying them in the sun, they can be dried in a hot-cupboard. When perfectly dry, store them in a well-covered tin.

Varhias are very tasty when curried with a few pieces of potato. They are used in making varhia pulāo, and one or two varhias can be added in the following curries:—fresh French beans, runner beans, broad beans, peas, marrow and leeks, but care should be taken to fry the varhias in the butter-fat with the onion mixture and cook in ½ teacupful of water before adding the other vegetables.

PHŪL-VARHIA

SMALL DRIED RICE PUFFS

½ pound fine ground rice
2 pints water
2 teaspoonfuls salt

1 teaspoonful baking powder
1-2 teaspoonfuls caraway seeds
(optional)

FOR 36 PHŪL-VARHIA. Sieve the ground rice, and keep it by you. Boil the water in a large thick aluminium saucepan; turn the heat low and mix in handfuls of ground rice, stirring all the time with a large spoon. Add salt, baking powder and the caraway seeds. Mix well for a minute or two, breaking up any lumps there may be; cover with a tight lid and keep it on the lowest possible heat for nearly an hour. Remove from heat; spread a clean teacloth on a large tray, and when the mixture is cool enough to handle, take about a tablespoonful and place it on the cloth, carefully keeping it in a round shape. Repeat the process until all the mixture is finished.

Leave these phūl-varhia to dry in the sun, or in a hot cupboard. If desired, the mixture can be shaped into long strips like cheese straws; but you will need to rub in a little edible oil to prevent the mixture sticking to your hand.

When they are thoroughly dried, store them in a tin. Phül-varhia should be fried quickly in deep smoking fat or oil just before serving. They rise to double or treble their original size, and are crisp and very tasty to serve at tea-time.

PĀPARHS

PUPPADUMS MADE WITH DĀL URHAD
OR RED LENTIL FLOUR

½ *lb. fine dāl urhad (see page 22) or red lentil flour*

1 *level dessertspoonful baking powder*

1 *teaspoonful caraway seeds*

1 *teaspoonful crushed cardamom seeds*

½ *teacupful warm water*

1 *teaspoonful salt*

1 *teaspoonful or more of crushed (not ground) black pepper*

1 *teaspoonful chilli powder (optional)*

2 *tablespoonfuls, or more, of edible oil or warm fat*

FOR 15 PĀPARHS. First set aside about a dessertspoonful of the flour for use later on, then place the remainder of the flour in a mixing bowl, and add salt. Mix the baking powder in the water, (in India we use a kind of cooking soda), and gradually add this to the flour, and mix into a stiff dough. Place this dough on a bread-board, pound it vigorously with a pestle for 15 minutes, using generous dabs of edible oil to prevent sticking. The expert pāparh makers bang the dough on the board as if threshing corn. Mix in the spices, chilli powder, etc., and pound once again. Indeed, the more you pound it, the lighter will be the pāparhs. Shape the whole of the dough into a long sausage, then cut into small portions. Place these and the remainder of the flour in a bowl, and get them well covered with the flour

How to shape the pāparhs

Take a portion of the flour-covered dough, grease it slightly, and shape it round. Then roll it out as thin and round as possible (very thin indeed), using more oil if necessary. Roll out the rest of the portions likewise, place them all separately on a large cake rack, and dry them in the sun or in a hot cupboard. They will only take a few hours to dry, and should not be kept in the cupboard too long. They will always have a shiny, greasy surface, and should be stored in a covered tin. Pāparhs can be baked slowly on both sides on a gas ring (of course, a charcoal fire is best), or they can be fried in smoking oil or fat. They are crisp and crunchy, and are served with drinks, with main meals, or at tea-time. They can be made quite plain, i.e., you can leave out the spices if not wanted.

Pāparh making is an art in itself, and needs a lot of practice to get perfect results, but it is certainly worth trying.

PĀPARH SĀGUDĀNA
PUPPADUMS MADE WITH SAGO

½ lb. sago
½ teaspoonful ground pepper
(black or white)

1½ teaspoonfuls salt
1½ pints water

FOR 32 PUPPADUMS. Wash the sago in cold water once or twice, drain it well. Bring the water to boil in a large, heavy aluminium saucepan, and stir in the well-washed sago. Add salt and pepper, and cook slowly for 15 minutes, stirring all the time. The sago should by now be cooked and swollen, and can be removed from the heat.

Arrange a clean cloth on a large tray, and spread a heaped tablespoonful of the mixture in a thin round shape on the cloth.

Repeat the process until all the mixture is used. Dry these in
the same way as described in the previous recipe; but they take
much longer to dry, and should be carefully unstuck from the
cloth before really dry. If they do get stuck, dampen the cloth
from the back, and gently persuade them from it.

They must be thoroughly dry before storing. Apart from
this, they are very easy to make, and are fried in deep smoking
fat just before serving.

They are very light and crisp, and attractive looking; and
are great favourites with children.

Bread Varieties

Bread Varieties

CHAPĀTĪS

UNLEAVENED INDIAN WHOLEMEAL BREAD

2½ teacupfuls wholemeal flour   1 tablespoon set butter-fat
About 1 teacupful water   (optional)
1 teaspoonful salt

FOR 10 TO 12 CHAPĀTĪS. Sieve 2 teacupfuls of the flour into a mixing bowl (saving ½ teacupful of flour for shaping the chapātīs); add salt, and mix into a loose dough by gradually adding the water. Pound and knead with the hands for several minutes, for the more it is kneaded the lighter will be the bread. Leave the dough for at least one hour, then knead once again, and if necessary sprinkle a little more water on it. Shape the chapātīs by breaking off a small portion of the dough, shaping it into a ball, and with the help of a little dry flour, rolling it out thin and round like a pancake. Heat the 'tava' (the iron hot-plate) and grease it slightly. Flatten the chapātī by tossing it from one hand to the other, then place it on the hot-plate and bake on medium heat, first on one side (only slightly this time), and then the other. Turn again, and encourage it to rise by pressing the sides of the chapātī with a clean cloth; the chapātī usually comes right up like a balloon. It should be baked all round before removing from the hot-plate; the baking can be finished off under the hot grill after it has been partially baked on the hot-plate. All this has to be done fairly quickly, as too slow cooking will make the chapātīs go hard. If butter-fat is used, it should be warmed up and then spread sparingly with a spoon on one side of each chapāti.

Chapātis are good to eat (with or without butter) just as they are removed from the heat, still puffed up. For keeping them hot, it is best to pile one on top of the other, and wrap a cloth round them. Then this bundle can be placed in a deep receptacle, covered, and kept in a very low-heated oven.

Chapātis are the mainstay of the majority of Indian folk particularly of Punjabis, and it is surprising how much nourishment is derived from them. In addition, I must point out that dogs are very fond of them and thrive on them wonderfully well.

NOTE: The hot-plate or a griddle must be used for baking chapātis; the grill is not suitable.

MAKKĪ KĪ ROTĪ

BREAD MADE WITH MAIZE FLOUR

4 *teacupfuls maize flour*	1-1½ *teacupfuls water*
1½ *teaspoonfuls salt*	1 *dessertspoonful (or more) butter-fat*

FOR 5 OR 6 ROTĪS. Sieve the flour, which is of yellowish colour and rather coarse. The roughage should be kept for another use. Add salt, and separating enough flour for one roti, make it into a stiff dough by gradually adding a little of the water. Mix and knead for a little while, then shape the roti, thick and round, on your hand, and place it on the well-greased 'tava' (hot iron plate). Continue the flattening by pressing it all round with the palm of the hand, taking care not to break it. Cook fairly slowly on both sides; the edges of this roti being usually uneven. The warmed butter-fat can be thinly spread

on it when the roti is removed from the heat. The dough for each of the rotis is prepared separately as you go along.

Some people prefer to mix a little warm butter-fat and chopped methi (feenugreek) in the dough, the inclusion of which makes the roti even tastier.

Makki kī roti is served hot or warm, usually with sāg (mixed greens) and dahi (milk-curd), and is considered to be very nourishing.

Pure maize or millet flour is rather difficult to obtain in this country, but I have been able to get good maize flour from my corn merchant. Polenta, the maize flour, which can be bought in Italian shops in Soho, London, is quite suitable for making makki kī roti providing it is fine enough.

BĀJRĒ KĪ ROTĪ
BREAD MADE WITH MILLET FLOUR

This is prepared in the same way as makki kī roti, except that millet flour is used instead of maize. Bājrē kī roti can be made crisp and sweet by adding some warm butter-fat (1 table-spoonful) and 1 lb. demerara sugar, dissolved in the water before mixing with the dough.

KHAMĪRĪ MOTĪ ROTĪ
LEAVENED BREAD

For Khamīr (home-made yeast)

4 oz. plain flour
(not wholemeal)
2 tablespoonfuls slightly
warm curd

2 teaspoonfuls sugar
1 dozen black peppercorns
(whole)
2 tablespoonfuls warm water

Sift the flour into a basin. Add sugar, peppercorns and the milk-curd. Mix well with the warm water, beat for a few minutes and leave in a warm place for 18 hours.

For Bread

4 *teacupfuls flour* (*wholemeal or plain*)	*About* 1½ *teacupfuls warm water*
The khamīr (*home-made yeast*)	1 *teaspoonful sugar* (*optional*)
2 *teaspoonfuls salt*	

FOR 6 ROTĪs. Sift the flour in a mixing bowl; add yeast (the peppercorns can be taken out and used again) and sugar. Rub the mixture with the hands, and gradually add the warm water. Knead for several minutes. Cover with a cloth and leave in a warm place to rise. When the dough is nearly double its original size, it is ready. Using a little warm water, knead the dough again for a minute or two, then with the help of a little dry flour, shape each rotī on the palm of the hand, keeping it fairly thick and round. Place it on the already heated iron plate, and cook on medium heat, turning it once or twice. When nearly done, place on a toaster under the grill, and toast well on both sides. This bread can be fried in deep hot fat instead of baking. Also, after the dough has risen, some warm butter-fat or other seasoning can be added to it. Kamīrī rotī is easily digested, and is very tasty.

PARĀTHAS
PUFFED BREAD

2½ *teacupfuls wholemeal flour*	2 *tablespoonfuls* (3 *oz.*) *or*
About 1 *teacupful water*	*more set butter-fat*
½ *teaspoonful salt*	

FOR 10 PARĀTHAS. Use 2 teacupfuls of the flour (saving ½ teacupful for shaping the parāthas) and prepare the dough for the
parāthas as for chapātīs (see page 119), and let the dough stand.
Heat the butter-fat, and have it by you. Break off a piece of the
dough, shape it into a ball, and, with the help of a little dry
flour, roll it out (not too thin). Using a spoon, spread some
warm butter-fat on it, then fold it over, and spread a little
more butter-fat on the fresh layer. Do this two or three times,
and eventually roll the parātha out fairly thin, either round or
V-shaped. Grease the hot iron plate well, and put the parātha
on it; when one side is partially cooked, turn it and spread
butter-fat liberally on it; do the same to the other side. When
ready, the parāthas should be of golden-brown colour, and
well soaked in butter-fat.

They should be served piping hot with vegetable or meat
dishes.

PARĀTHAS STUFFED WITH
POTATO MIXTURE

For the Stuffing

2 *large potatoes*
1 *small onion*
2 *tablespoonfuls dhania, or*
  other fresh herbs
1 *dessertspoonful butter-fat*
1 *teaspoonful garam-masāla*
1½ *teaspoonfuls salt*

1 *tablespoonful ground mango*
  or 1 *dessertspoonful lemon*
  juice
A small piece of ginger, and
  ½ *teaspoonful chilli powder*
  (optional)

Boil the potatoes in their jackets; when cool, peel and mash
them. Heat the butter-fat in a frying pan, and fry the minced
or finely chopped onion, herbs and ginger slowly for a few

minutes. Add salt, garam-masāla, chilli powder and lemon
juice. Mix in the already prepared potatoes, and let sizzle for
two or three minutes. Remove from heat and allow to cool.

The ingredients and the preparation of the dough are the
same as for plain parāthas.

After rolling the parātha out—not too thinly—spread the
warm butter-fat on it as before, and place a tablespoonful or
more of the prepared potato mixture in the centre. Fold all
round, and then with the help of some dry flour, roll the
parātha out as thinly and round as you can. Cook the stuffed
parāthas in the same way as the plain ones.

These parāthas are very tasty eaten with dahi (milk-curd).

PARĀTHA STUFFED WITH PEAS

For the Stuffing

1½-2 *teacupfuls freshly
shelled peas*

1 *medium-sized tomato*

1-2 *tablespoonfuls broken-up
dhania, (see page 20), or
other fresh herbs*

A little ginger and ½ *a teaspoonful chilli powder*

1 *medium-sized onion*

1 *dessertspoonful butter-fat*

1-1½ *teaspoonfuls salt*

1 *teaspoonful garam-masāla*

1 *dessertspoonful ground
mango or lemon juice
(optional)*

Put the butter-fat in a saucepan, and fry in it gently the minced
or finely chopped onion, ginger and the herbs. Add sliced
tomatoes, salt, garam-masāla and chilli powder, mix well, and
then add the washed and well-drained peas. Let these sizzle
for a few minutes, cover and cook on a low heat until peas are
tender. The superfluous liquid can be dried off by turning the
heat higher. Mash the peas slightly, add the lemon juice, and
use when cool.

PARĀTHAS STUFFED WITH CAULIFLOWER

For the Stuffing

1½-2 teacupfuls finely grated
   cauliflower
1 teaspoonful garam-masāla
1-1½ teaspoonfuls salt

¼ oz. grated ginger (fresh or
   dried)
and ½ teaspoonful chilli
   powder (optional)

Finely grate only the flower part and the very tender stalks of
the cauliflower (the rest can be kept for another use). Place the
grated cauliflower on a large plate, mix in the rest of the
ingredients, and stuff the parāthas with this mixture immediately. This stuffing cannot be prepared in advance.

PARĀTHAS STUFFED WITH INDIAN, CHINESE, OR ORDINARY RADISHES

For the Stuffing

1-1½ teacupfuls grated
   radishes
¼ oz. root ginger (fresh or
   dried)
½ teaspoonful chilli powder

1½-2 teaspoonfuls salt
1-2 teaspoonfuls garam-
   masāla
1 tablespoonful dried and
   crushed pomegranate seeds

Thoroughly wash, drain and grate the radishes, and squeeze
the superfluous juice out of them. Add grated ginger and the
rest of the ingredients. Stuff the parāthas with this mixture
immediately, because this stuffing becomes too watery if prepared in advance.

The large red or white Chinese radishes, when in season,
are obtainable in this country. Ordinary large radishes can be
used, if desired.

Indian radishes are generally white and are sometimes even larger than carrots. We have not been able to grow them here. Chinese radishes, however, can be grown here.

These parāthas are usually eaten with thick dahi (milk-curd).

PŪRIS
INDIAN FRIED BREAD

3 *teacupfuls wholemeal flour*   *About* 1¼ *teacupfuls warm*
1 *dessertspoonful butter-fat*   *water*
½ *lb. fat, or its equivalent in*   1 *teaspoonful salt*
  oil, for frying

FOR 14 TO 18 PŪRIS. Sieve the flour in a large mixing bowl, heat the butter-fat and add that and the salt, rub in with your hands, and then make all into a stiff dough by gradually adding the warm water. Knead for a few minutes.

To shape the Pūris

Take a little of the dough, make into a ball, then with the help of a little dry flour roll it out round and fairly thin. Repeat the process until all the pūris are rolled out; keep them separate from each other. Using a deep karhāi or chip pan, heat the oil or fat to nearly smoking point and fry each pūri separately fairly quickly on medium heat. Encourage it to rise by slightly pressing the sides with the slice or turner after the pūri is partially cooked, and by splashing some of the hot fat in the pan on top of it. When the pūri has risen (some only rise slightly), and is golden brown on both sides, it is ready. Drain well and place on a warm, shallow dish. After they have been fried, the pūris can be kept warm in a very low oven. They are usually eaten hot, though in summer some people like them cold or merely warm. They are eaten with most of the Indian dishes, particularly with semolina halva, kabli channas, and dry potato curry.

KHAMĪRĪ PŪRĪ

INDIAN FRIED BREAD, LEAVENED

4 oz. plain flour
  (not wholemeal)
1½ teaspoonfuls sugar
½ teaspoonful salt
Some oil or fat for frying

1 tablespoonful home-made
  khamīr yeast (see page 121)
1 teaspoonful set butter-fat
½ teacupful warm milk

FOR 6 PŪRĪS. Sieve the flour in a mixing bowl, add yeast, salt, sugar, and the warmed-up butter-fat. Mix into a dough by gradually adding the warm milk. Knead for several minutes, and leave in a warm place for 2 to 3 hours. Then, with the help of a little warm water, knead the dough again. Divide into six, and roll each section into small round pūrīs (not too thin), and fry them in deep fat on medium heat.

These pūrīs are light, and very delicious.

KHASTA PŪRĪ

ANOTHER VARIETY OF FRIED BREAD

1½ teacupfuls wholemeal flour
1 teacupful self-raising flour
1 teaspoonful set butter-fat
Some oil or fa 1for frying

1 teaspoonful salt
Just over ½ teacupful warm
  water

FOR 10 PŪRĪS. Sieve the flour and mix in the butter-fat and salt. Gradually add the warm water and mix into a stiff dough, knead for several minutes and then leave covered for 15 minutes. Break off a small portion of the dough, and after shaping it into a ball, roll it out fairly thin and round. Repeat until the dough is finished. Heat the oil or fat in a chip pan, and when smoking hot, fry each pūrī separately in it, fairly quickly, turning frequently so that the pūrīs are well fried on both sides. When they are of an almond brown colour, drain them well and place in a shallow dish. Serve them hot.

Pūrīs usually rise up like a balloon, and are very tasty eaten with various Indian dishes.

PŪRĪ WITH POTATO PASTRY

2 *medium-sized potatoes*
　(*about 8 oz. after peeling
　and cooking*)
8 *oz. plain flour* (*not whole-
　meal*)

2 *teaspoonfuls salt*
½ *teacupful warm water*
Some oil or fat for frying

FOR 14 TO 15 PŪRĪS. Boil the potatoes in their jackets, and remove from heat when just tender. Allow to cool, and after skinning them mash thoroughly. Knead them for a few minutes, sieve in the flour, add salt and rub the mixture with your hands, making it into a stiff pastry by gradually adding the warm water. Knead and roll again as for ordinary pūrīs. Heat the fat or oil in a chip pan and fry each pūrī separately on *medium* heat, encouraging them to rise by spooning the hot fat over them. When golden brown on both sides, drain the pūrīs and place on a shallow dish.

These pūrīs can be served hot or cold, and are very delicious when eaten with kabli channas or curried haricot or other dried beans.

LUCHCHĪ

ANOTHER VARIETY OF FRIED BREAD

4 oz. plain flour
(not wholemeal)
½ oz. butter-fat
1 teaspoonful salt

*Nearly ½ teacupful warm
water
Some oil or fat for frying*

FOR 6 OR 7 LUCHCHĪS. Sieve the flour into a mixing bowl, and rub in the fat. Add salt, and make into a very stiff pastry by adding the warm water. Pound and knead for several minutes. Divide the pastry into 6 or 7 portions, shape these into balls, and roll each one out—with the help of a little dry flour—very thin and round. Get them all ready, and then fry them separately and fairly quickly in deep hot fat. Drain them thoroughly, and serve warm or cold.

KACHŌRHĪS

STUFFED PŪRĪS

The pastry for kachōrhīs is prepared in the same way and with the same ingredients as for plain pūrīs (page 126). They are rolled out slightly thicker and smaller, and after stuffing with the following mixtures, are fried as ordinary pūrīs.

They can be stuffed with the potato, lentil or peas mixtures, as given in the recipe for stuffed parāthas (pages 123-5).

LUCHCHI
ANOTHER VARIETY OF FRIED BREAD

4 oz. plain flour	Nearly 1 teacupful sour
(or ½ bakwheat)	water
4 oz. butter-fat	Some oil or fat for frying
1 teaspoonful salt	

For 6 or 7 LUCHCHIS. Sieve the flour into a mixing-bowl and rub in the fat. Add salt, and make into a very stiff pastry by adding the warm water. Pound and knead for several minutes. Divide the pastry into 6 or 7 portions, shape these into balls, and roll each one out—with the help of a little dry flour—very thin and round. Get them all ready, and then fry them separately and fairly quickly in deep hot fat. Drain them thoroughly, and serve warm or cold.

KACHORHIS
STUFFED PURIS

The pastry for kachorhis is prepared in the same way and with the same ingredients as for plain puris (page 120). They are rolled out slightly thicker and smaller, and after stuffing with the following mixtures, are fried as ordinary puris.

They can be stuffed with the potato, lentil or peas mixtures, as given in the recipe for stuffed parathas (pages 124-5).

Milk-Curd Preparations

Milk-Curd Preparations

DAHI BARHĒ

SAVOURY LENTIL RISSOLES IN CURD

2 *pints fresh thick milk-curd*	1 *teacupful dāl urhad, moong*
1 *teaspoonful garam-masāla*	*(page 22) or red lentils*
1½-2 *teaspoonfuls salt*	1 *dessertspoonful chopped mint*
1 *teaspoonful chilli powder*	*or onions*
1 *teaspoonful caraway seeds*	*Some oil or fat for frying*

Wash and soak the pulses in plenty of water overnight. Drain
well the next day, and crush and pound them in a pestle and
mortar a little at a time, as when making monghōris (page 110).
Mix 1 teaspoonful of salt and ½ teaspoonful caraway seeds with
the crushed pulses. Using a chip pan, bring the oil or fat to
nearly smoking point; take a little of the mixture, flatten it
slightly and on medium heat fry three or four rissoles at a time,
until they are of a light brown colour on both sides. When all
are done, rinse them in cold water to soften and get thoroughly
cold.

Whisk the milk-curd, place it in a glass or china dish, add
the remainder of the salt, garam-masāla, caraway seeds, chilli
powder and the chopped mint. Squeeze and flatten the rissoles
and put them in the curd mixture. They should be ready to
serve after 15 minutes. To improve the appearance of this dish,
some people sprinkle a little ground paprika (which is not 'hot'
at all) on the top.

This dish is served cold and tamarind chutney is often
served with it.

DAHI CARHI I

A CURD PREPARATION SIMILAR TO SOUP

For Pakoris

2-3 *tablespoonfuls besan or split-pea flour*

2-3 *tablespoonfuls warm water*

½ *teaspoon salt*

½ *teaspoonful garam-masāla*

Some oil or fat for frying

For Curry

2 *teacupfuls curd which has been kept for a day or two, or lassi (whey)*

2 *tablespoonfuls besan or split-pea flour*

1 *tablespoonful (1½ oz.) set butter-fat*

1-1½ *teaspoonfuls salt*

1 *teaspoonful garam-masāla*

1 *teaspoonful turmeric*

1 *to 2 fresh green chillis or ½ teaspoonful chilli powder (if desired)*

1 *teacupful milk*

1 *teacupful water*

1 *doz. small spring onions*

2 *tablespoonfuls broken-up dhania or other herbs*

1 *teaspoonful caraway seeds*

To make pakoris

Sieve 2-3 tablespoonfuls of besan or split-pea flour into a small mixing bowl; add salt and garam-masāla, and make into a thick batter by gradually adding the warm water. Beat hard and allow to stand for a few minutes. Heat the fat or oil in a chip pan to nearly boiling point. Beat the batter once again, and taking some of it in your hand, drop small portions into the hot fat. Fry as many as you can at a time on medium heat: keep them on the move, and when they are a golden brown colour, take them from the pan and drain. Repeat the process until all the mixture is used up.

To make the curry

Using a saucepan, fry gently in the butter-fat the onions, herbs and the green chillis (if using them). Add turmeric and salt, and after a few minutes add the already prepared pakoris. Let these sizzle for 2 or 3 minutes.

Sieve the two tablespoonfuls of besan into a small bowl, add a little of the water and make into a batter. Gradually add the rest of the water and milk and the well-beaten curd or lassi (whey). If the curd is not tart enough, 1 tablespoonful of lemon juice should be added to the mixture. Pour this liquid onto the sizzling pakoris, bring to boil and then turn heat to medium. Keep stirring until the curry thickens, then continue cooking gently for 20 or 30 minutes. Add garam-masāla and caraway seeds before removing from the heat.

The flavour of dahi carhi is improved by keeping it in a low heated oven for a little while after it has been cooked. It is usually served hot, and goes well with rice pulāo.

DAHI CARHI II

A CURD PREPARATION SIMILAR TO SOUP

2 teacupfuls curd which has been kept for a day or two

1 teacupful milk

1 teacupful water

2 tablespoonfuls besan (split-pea flour) or 1½ tablespoonfuls cornflour

1 tablespoonful (1½ oz.) set butter-fat

5 small potatoes

6 small onions

2 medium-sized capsicums (sweet peppers, optional)

2 tablespoonfuls broken-up dhania or other herbs

1½ teaspoonfuls salt

1 teaspoonful turmeric

1 teaspoonful garam-masāla

1 teaspoonful caraway seeds (optional)

1 teaspoonful chilli powder (optional)

FOR 4 OR 5 PEOPLE. Sieve the split-pea flour or cornflour into a mixing bowl, and make into a thin paste with some of the water. Mix in the milk, the milk-curd and the rest of the water. Keep this in a jug. Using a saucepan, fry in the butter-fat the onions, thick pieces of sweet peppers and the well-scraped potatoes, for a few minutes. Add turmeric, salt, herbs, caraway seeds and the chilli powder; cover the saucepan and cook gently until the vegetables are tender. Then add the curd mixture from the jug, bring to the boil and keep stirring until the curry thickens. After that, it can either be cooked, well covered, on a low heat for 30 to 40 minutes, or better still, it can be placed with the lid on in the oven (Regulo 5) for the same length of time. Mix in the garam-masāla about ten minutes before removing from the heat.

If the curd is not tart enough, a tablespoonful of lemon juice can be added to the curd mixture. Also, for a change, a few pieces of cauliflower, or varhia (dried lentil cakes) can be used instead of potatoes, but whatever you put in, it must be allowed to get tender before adding the curd mixture.

This dish should be served piping hot, and goes very well with savoury rice pulāo.

RAITA ALU

POTATOES IN CURD

2 *pints fresh thick curd*	1 *teaspoonful garam-masāla*
2 *large potatoes*	1 *teaspoonful chilli powder*
1½ *teaspoonfuls caraway*	*(optional)*
seeds	1½ *teaspoonfuls salt*

FOR 8 PEOPLE. Boil the potatoes in their jackets. When cool, skin them and cut into fairly small pieces. Beat the curd, and

mix in the rest of the ingredients. Put in the potatoes, mix well with a spoon.

Rāita is always served cold—indeed if it could be placed in a refrigerator for a short time before using the flavour would be improved.

RĀITA MINT AND ONION

Made as raīta ālū, with the addition of 3 medium-sized onions, finely sliced, and 3 tablespoonfuls of coarsely chopped mint.

RĀITA CUCUMBER

Made as rāita ālū, with the addition of 1 medium-sized cucumber, raw and grated.

RĀITA MARROW

Ingredients as for rāita ālū, with the addition of 1 small marrow. Marrow to be peeled, grated, slightly boiled, cooled down and squeezed before adding to the curd mixture. Any large seeds should be removed, if too hard.

RĀITA AUBERGINE

Ingredients as for rāita ālū, with the addition of 3 medium-sized aubergines.

Place the aubergines under a grill or toaster, or over the gas-ring; turn frequently, and when their skins turn black and they are soft inside, place under running water and carefully peel by hand. When cool, mash well and put into the curd mixture.

RĀITA PAKORI

SAVOURY DROPS IN CURD

For pakoris

4 tablespoonfuls besan   ¾ teacupful water
  (split-pea flour)   Some frying oil
1 teaspoonful salt

Other ingredients as for rāita ālū

FOR 8 PEOPLE. Make a thick batter of the ingredients, beat well
and allow to stand for ten minutes. Bring the oil to boiling
point in a deep frying pan. Place some batter on a slice with
large round holes and shake through holes into the pan. Keep
the pakoris on the move whilst frying, and when they are of a
golden-brown colour, remove and allow to drain while a new
batch is cooking. When cold, soften with tepid water and put
into the curd mixture.

SWEET RĀITAS

RĀITA BANANA

5-6 ripe yellow bananas   3-4 tablespoonfuls sugar
2 pints fresh milk-curd   (preferably caster)

FOR 8 PEOPLE. Beat the curd and place it in a glass dish. Peel
and cut the bananas into thin round pieces and put them in the
curd. Stir in sugar, and serve either as an after-dinner sweet
or as ordinary rāita

RĀITA SULTANAS

2 *pints fresh milk-curd*   3-4 *tablespoonfuls sugar*
4-6 *tablespoonfuls sultanas*   (*preferably caster*)

FOR 8 PEOPLE. Wash and soak the sultanas for nearly 30 minutes
before putting them in the well-beaten milk-curd. Add sugar,
and serve in the same way as banana rāita.

Sweetmeats

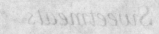

Sweetmeats

LADDOO BOONDI

For mixture, etc.

1½ teacupfuls (4 oz.) besan
 or fine split-pea flour
 (weighed after sieving)
¼ teaspoonful saffron
 (for colour and fragrance)
1 dessertspoonful desiccated
 coconut
1 dessertspoonful finely sliced
 pistachio kernels or
 almond nuts

Just over ½ teacupful milk and
 water mixed
½ teaspoonful cardamom seeds
 (not crushed), or grated
 nutmeg
9 oz. butter-fat, or any other
 clarified fat

For syrup

Just over 1½ teacupfuls
 (12 oz.) sugar
1½ teacupfuls water

Three slices or turners will be
 needed, with medium-sized
 holes.

FOR 20 MEDIUM-SIZED LADDOOS. Place the sieved flour in a small mixing bowl. Soak the saffron in a dessertspoonful of water, and mix half of this in the flour. Gradually add the warm milk and water, mixing it into a thick batter, which will feel more like cake-mixture than batter. Beat hard for several minutes. The mixture should be able to drop easily, but should not be too thin. Leave it for ten to fifteen minutes.

To make the syrup

Using a spacious saucepan, mix the sugar and water together, and boil fairly quickly for 8 minutes. Test by dropping a little of it on a plate—if it forms into a still ball then it is ready. Add the rest of the saffron, and keep it by you, on the lowest possible heat.

To fry the boondi

Using a deep chip pan, put 8 oz. of the butter-fat in it (keeping 1 oz. for mixing-in afterwards), and bring to nearly smoking point. To test the temperature, it is best to fry one or two drops of mixture first. Using one of the turners or slices, place about a tablespoonful of the mixture on it, and tap the slice on the inside edges of the pan to make the mixture fall through the holes into the hot fat. This boondi should be fried fairly quickly, and as soon as one batch is done, put it in the syrup. Keep moving the soaked boondi to the sides of the saucepan, and if the syrup is too dry, sprinkle a little hot water on it. When all the mixture has been used, and the boondi is in the syrup, mix thoroughly with one of the slices, and add nuts and cardamom seeds.

Heat the remaining 1 oz. of butter-fat, and pour it on the mixture. When slightly cool, form into balls or laddoos by taking some of this mixed boondi, pressing it hard, then shaping it by shifting from one hand to the other and pressing hard all the time.

Laddoo boondi are a traditional Indian sweetmeat, and are a great favourite with grown-ups and children alike. No Indian feast is complete without them.

NOTE: Saffron, which can be obtained from your local chemist, should be in the form of small fragments.

LADDOO SŪJI

SEMOLINA LADDOO

4 oz. very fine semolina
4 oz. set butter-fat
4 oz. caster sugar
1 teaspoonful cardamom seeds
  or nutmeg

1 tablespoonful, or more, of
finely sliced almonds or other
nuts

FOR 12 TO 14 LADDOOS. Using a thick aluminium saucepan, fry the semolina in the butter-fat quite slowly for about 15 minutes. When the fat seems to separate from the semolina, and the sweet fragrance starts to come from it, then it is ready. Care should be taken not to let the semolina get brown. Remove from heat, cool slightly, add sugar and mix thoroughly with a spoon: add the cardamom seeds or nutmeg and the finely sliced nuts. Mix once more, and when the mixture is fairly cold, form into small balls or laddoos.

The above method is also used for laddoo besan.

PINNIS—MADE WITH WHOLEMEAL FLOUR AND KHOYA

2 oz. khoya, or full-cream
  powdered milk
6 oz. caster sugar
4 oz. wholemeal flour
4 oz. set butter-fat
1½ tablespoonfuls sultanas

1 tablespoonful desiccated
coconut
1-2 tablespoonfuls finely sliced
almonds or other nuts
1 teaspoonful crushed cardamom seeds or grated nutmeg

FOR 15 TO 20 PINNIS. Fry the flour in the butter-fat in the same way as in the previous recipe. Allow to cool slightly, then add caster sugar and khoya. If full-cream powdered milk is used, it should be mixed with about 1½ tablespoonfuls of water (hot), and beaten until it is like stiff pastry before mixing in with the fried flour and sugar. Add nuts and sultanas, and mix thoroughly. Form into pinnis of the desired size, which will keep for several days.

Pinnis are slightly flatter than laddoos.

PINNIS MADE WITH DĀL OR LENTIL MIXTURE

1 teacupful *dāl urhad* (see page 22) *or red lentils*	1½ tablespoonfuls desiccated coconut
8 oz. *butter-fat*	½ to 1 teaspoonful separated cardamom seeds *or grated nutmeg*
2 tablespoonfuls sliced pistachio *or almond nuts*	
10 oz. *sugar* (preferably *caster*)	

FOR 20 PINNIS. Soak the dāl urhad or lentils overnight, then drain them well and leave to dry slightly for a little while. Then, using a pestle and mortar, crush and pound them, a little at a time, until they almost resemble cake mixture. Using an aluminium saucepan, fry this mixture fairly slowly in the butter-fat for 8 to 10 minutes. Remove from heat, scrape from the sides and bottom, and continue stirring until it is half cold. Add sugar, nuts (saving some of them for top decorating), and the cardamom seeds, mix thoroughly and leave until quite cold. Then, taking a little of the mixture, form each pinni (slightly flatter than laddoos), and place on a shallow, buttered dish: repeating the process until all the pinnis are formed, then decorating on top with sliced nuts. They will be set and ready to serve after an hour or so.

These pinnis are considered very nourishing, and are especially recommended for convalescents.

GULĀB JĀMANS

A SYRUPY SWEETMEAT

2½ pints milk (preferably Jersey milk)
1 tablespoonful lemon juice
1 teaspoonful plain or self-raising flour
1½ teacupfuls sugar

1½ teacupfuls water
1 tablespoonful rosewater
2 dozen small pistachio kernels or almonds
6 to 8 oz. of fat, for frying

FOR 18 GULĀB JĀMANS. Make panīr (soft milk 'cheese', see page 19) in the usual way by using 1 pint of milk: make khoya (condensed milk, see page 20) with the remainder of the milk.

Mix panīr, khoya and flour together, pound and knead well until the mixture is smooth and feels like stiff pastry. Take a small portion of this pastry, shape it into a narrow sausage 1½ to 2 inches long, break in half and place a very small nut, or part of one, between, and then press and shape together again. Make as many gulāb jāmans this way as the mixture will furnish, and have them ready for cooking.

Put the sugar and water in a saucepan and boil quickly for seven minutes. When the syrup is sticky (not too stiff) leave it on a very low heat. Put the fat in a chip pan, and when it is hot (not quite smoking) fry the gulāb jāmans 4 or 5 at a time in the deep fat, quite slowly, turning them just once. When they have risen, and are of almond brown colour, take them out of the fat, drain and put them in the warm syrup: repeating the process until all are made. Remove from heat, and empty gulāb jāmans and syrup into a dish, and when cool, add the rosewater.

Gulāb jāmans are served warm or cold with a little of the syrup. They are a well-known Indian sweetmeat, and a great favourite, either as an after-dinner sweet, or at tea-time. They can be made entirely of khoya, instead of khoya and panīr, the rest of the ingredients being the same.

GULĀB JĀMAN, WITH KHOYA AND POTATO PASTRY

1½ *pints milk* (*preferably the half-pint to be Jersey milk*)
1 *tablespoonful self-raising flour* (*not wholemeal*)
1 *tablespoonful rosewater*

3 *medium-sized potatoes* (*which should make 4 oz. potato pastry*)
½ *teaspoonful crushed cardamom seeds or grated nutmeg*

For syrup, etc.

½ *lb. sugar*
8 *oz. of fat, for frying*

1½ *teacupfuls water*

FOR 14 GULĀB JĀMANS. Boil the potatoes in their jackets, and when cooked (not broken), cool and carefully skin them, then mash and knead. Using a thick aluminium frying pan, mix milk and the potato pastry together, and boil fairly quickly for an hour, scraping frequently from the bottom and sides until the mixture is quite thick. Then stir vigorously and dry out all the superfluous liquid. Remove from heat, and turn the mixture onto a plate. When slightly cold, mix in the flour and the crushed cardamom seeds or grated nutmeg.

Shape the gulāb jamans in the same way as in the previous gulāb jaman recipe, except that the pieces of nuts are not placed in the centre of each one.

To make the syrup

Using a large saucepan, mix sugar and water together and boil quickly for 6 to 8 minutes. The syrup should be quite sticky, but not too stiff. Keep it warm on the lowest possible heat.

Fry the gulāb jāmans three or four at a time in deep, hot fat on rather less than medium heat, and not too slowly. When they are fairly brown on both sides, take them out and put into the syrup. When all are done, bring the syrup to the boil with the gulāb jāmans in it. Care must be taken not to crush them: a slice or turner (not a spoon) should be used for shifting and turning them.

When slightly cool, put them—syrup and all—in a glass dish, and add rosewater. Serve them warm or cold.

They are delicious, and the adding of the potato pastry seems to make them tastier still.

RASGULLAS
ANOTHER VARIETY OF SYRUPY SWEETMEAT

3 *pints of milk*	1½ *tablespoonfuls of rosewater*
3 *tablespoonfuls slightly warm*	*for flavouring*
lemon juice, or 1½ *teacup-*	1 *dessertspoonful very fine*
fuls milk-curd	*semolina*
2 *teacupfuls sugar*	12 *small pieces broken-up*
4 *teacupfuls water*	*lump sugar*

To make panir (soft milk 'cheese')

FOR 10 TO 12 RASGULLAS. Boil the milk, stirring continuously to prevent skin forming on top. As the milk comes up to the boil, add the slightly warmed lemon juice or curd, and bring to boil. When solid lumps have formed, strain off through a muslin bag, place bag on a clean board and press with fairly heavy weight to get rid of all liquid.

To prepare rasgullas

Empty the panīr onto a clean board, add fine semolina, and pound and knead until it starts to become greasy. From this, form 12 round balls. Break each ball in half and place a small piece of sugar between, then press and shape together again.

To make the syrup

Mix sugar and water together, boil for seven minutes on medium heat. Take out 1½ teacupfuls of this thin syrup and keep it by you.

Place the rasgullas into the syrup remaining in the saucepan, bring quickly to boil, then turn heat low, and keep boiling gently (uncovered), shaking saucepan frequently. Gradually add the syrup previously taken out, so that the rasgullas are being cooked in *thin* syrup all the time. This will take about an hour and a quarter, and when ready, rasgullas should be well swollen and the syrup whitish looking. Remove from heat, and after partly cooling, add rosewater.

Rasgullas are served warm or cold, with a little of the syrup. They are a well-known Indian sweetmeat, and a great favourite, either as an after-dinner sweet or at tea-time. Some people pour some cream or rabarhi (see page 37) over them before serving.

JALEBIS
CURLY SWEETMEAT

1½ teacupfuls plain flour	1 teaspoonful saffron
2 tablespoonfuls milk-curd	(optional)
1 teacupful warm water	1 pint of oil or fat for frying
	A medium-sized bakelite funnel

For syrup

2 *teacupfuls sugar*   2 *teacupfuls water*

FOR 18 JALEBIS. Sieve the flour into a basin, and by gradually adding the curd and water make it into a thick batter. Add the saffron, and beat hard for several minutes. Let this stand overnight in a warm place.

Make the syrup by boiling the sugar and water together on medium heat for 7 to 10 minutes. The syrup should be quite sticky but not stiff, and be kept at tepid heat while waiting to use.

Heat the fat in a deep frying pan to nearly smoking point, then fill the bakelite funnel with the well-beaten batter, remove finger and shape each jalebi as the batter pours into the fat by moving the funnel round three or four times at one place to make a curly ring about the size of a small pineapple ring. Fry three or four at a time, and when golden brown on both sides, drain on a slice with holes in it, and dip in the syrup. When they have soaked up sufficient syrup, place them in a row on a large shallow dish.

Jalebis are a well-known Indian sweetmeat, and can be served hot or cold. Some people like them soaked in milk.

SANDESH

SWEETMEAT MADE WITH SOFT MILK CHEESE

3 *pints fresh milk*
3 *tablespoonfuls lemon juice,*
   or 1½ teacupfuls milk-curd
7 *oz. sugar*

2 *dozen or more pistachio*
   kernels or other nuts
1 *teaspoonful, or more,*
   crushed cardamom seeds or
   grated nutmeg

FOR 10 OR 12 PIECES. Heat the milk in a heavy saucepan, and when it comes to the boil, add lemon juice or the milk-curd. Keep on a low heat for a minute or two, and stir until solid lumps are formed. Strain into a muslin bag, and leaving it on a board, press with heavy weight for 15 minutes or longer. Shred this panir into a heavy aluminium saucepan, add sugar, and place on a low heat. Stir well for 10 minutes or so. It will loosen at first, and then thicken up. When fairly thick, remove from heat, and turn the mixture into small diamond-shaped tins. Decorate each one with finely-sliced kernels and the crushed cardamom seeds or grated nutmeg. When thoroughly cold, take them carefully out of the tins.

If tins are not available, spread the mixture thickly on a shallow plate, and decorate. When half-cold, cut into diamond-shaped pieces, but do not separate them until they are almost cold.

This sweetmeat is very delicious, and quite easy to make.

MASŪR PĀK I
MYSORE SWEETMEAT

6 *oz. butter-fat, clarified margarine, or a mixture of the two*	1 *dessertspoonful ground almonds*
2 *heaped tablespoonfuls besan or fine split-pea flour**	1-2 *tablespoonfuls sliced almonds*
8 *oz. sugar*	1 *teaspoonful crushed cardamom seeds or any other sweet flavouring*
½ *teacupful water*	

FOR 15 PIECES. Keep near you the sliced almonds, crushed cardamom seeds and the ground almonds. Take out nearly 2 oz. butter-fat, warm it and keep it to use later on. Place the

* Plain Flour (not wholemeal) can be used in place of Besan or split-pea flour.

rest of the butter-fat or margarine-fat in a thick aluminium frying pan, and let it melt.

Sieve the flour and gradually add it to the simmering fat. Fry gently for 4-5 minutes, then add the ground almonds and the flavouring. Keep it on very low heat. Mix sugar and water and boil for 4 minutes on medium heat, by which time the syrup should be quite sticky. Pour this over the frying flour: mix quickly, and fry on medium heat for 7-8 minutes, adding a dessertspoonful of warm butter-fat after every two minutes, and stirring continuously. The mixture then should be quite thick and of slightly spongy appearance. Spread it thickly on a shallow dish and decorate soon afterwards, because this mixture dries very quickly.

When half cold, carefully cut into diamond-shaped pieces.

This sweetmeat is also a well-known one, and very easy to make.

MASŪR PĀK II

6 oz. butter-fat, clarified margarine, or a mixture of the two	1 dessertspoonful ground almonds
2 heaped tablespoonfuls besan or fine split-pea flour	1-2 tablespoonfuls sliced almonds
8 oz. sugar	1 teaspoonful crushed carda-mom seeds or any other
1 teacupful water	sweet flavouring

Place all the butter-fat, sugar and water in a heavy frying pan. Boil these on medium heat for about 8 minutes. Turn heat lower, and in this sizzling mixture mix the well-sieved besan flour little by little, and stir vigorously. Add ground almonds. Keep stirring for 5 to 6 minutes, when the mixture should be fairly thick and spongy.

Spread thickly on a dish, decorate, and soon afterwards cut carefully into desired pieces.

SOHAN HALVA
CONDENSED MILK SWEETMEAT

4 oz. khoya (home-made
condensed milk) (see
page 20) or khoya
made with powdered milk

1 to 2 dozen pistachio or
almond nuts

1 teaspoonful crushed
cardamom seeds or grated
nutmeg

6 oz. sugar

4 oz. butter-fat

1 to 2 tablespoonfuls sliced
mixed nuts

WILL MAKE 12 SQUARES. Place the khoya in a thick aluminium
saucepan. Add 3 oz. of butter-fat, and let it cook gently for
4 to 5 minutes, stirring frequently. Add the sugar, stir vigorously, keeping the heat at medium until the mixture is fairly
thick, which should not take more than ten minutes. Remove
from the heat, and spread the mixture on a buttered dish, and
decorate with sliced nuts. Heat the remainder of the butter-fat,
and pour over it. Allow to get cool, and then cut into pieces of
the desired size.

This is a very delicious sweetmeat, and will retain its flavour
for several weeks, particularly if it is made with home-made
condensed milk khoya.

CARROT SWEETMEAT

1½ pints fresh milk

¼ lb. freshly grated carrots

5 oz. sugar

2 tablespoonfuls (3 oz.) set
butter-fat

2 tablespoonfuls well-washed
sultanas (optional)

1 teaspoonful crushed
cardamom seeds or grated
nutmeg

1 teaspoonful desiccated
coconut

2 tablespoonfuls finely sliced
mixed nuts

FOR 15 SQUARES. Using a large, heavy aluminium frying pan, put the milk and grated carrots to boil on medium heat. Keep boiling until the mixture thickens, stirring frequently. This should take about 45 minutes. Add sugar and keep stirring for another 15 minutes, then add the butter-fat. Turn the heat a little lower, and keep frying and mixing until most of the fat has been absorbed in the mixture: this should take less than ten minutes. Add the sultanas and mix thoroughly. Remove from heat, and pour the sweetmeat onto a shallow, buttered dish. Spread it thickly, and decorate with desiccated coconut, mixed nuts and the crushed cardamom seeds.

When cool, cut into pieces of the desired size.

This sweetmeat is very tasty and nourishing.

ALMOND SWEETMEAT WITH FULL-CREAM POWDERED MILK

¾ *pint fresh milk*	2 *oz. full-cream powdered*
1½ *oz. ground almonds*	*milk*
2 *dozen almond nuts*	1 *teaspoonful crushed*
5 *oz. sugar*	*cardamom seeds or grated*
	nutmeg

FOR 15 SMALL PIECES. Using a heavy aluminium frying pan, boil the fresh milk; add the ground almonds and boil fairly quickly until the mixture thickens. This should not take more than 20 minutes. Add the powdered milk and cook gently for 5-7 minutes. Add the sugar, mix well and keep on medium heat for another 10 minutes. The mixture should now be fairly thick. Remove onto a well-buttered shallow dish, and spread out evenly.

Decorate with peeled and sliced almonds and cardamom seeds or nutmeg. Cut into shapes when almost cold.

COCONUT SWEETMEAT I

1 *teacupful finely desiccated coconut*	1 *teaspoonful crushed cardamom seeds or grated*
1½ *pints milk*	*nutmeg*
1 *dessertspoonful coarse desiccated coconut or fresh grated coconut*	½ *lb. sugar*
	A few pieces of edible silver leaf or silver balls

FOR 16 TO 18 SQUARES. Boil the milk in a heavy aluminium frying pan, mix in the coconut and boil for just over 30 minutes, when the mixture should be quite thick. Add sugar, and keep cooking and stirring for another 10 to 15 minutes until there is no superfluous milk left in the sweetmeat. Pour onto a well buttered dish, and decorate with the coarse desiccated coconut, cardamom seeds and the strips of edible silver leaf (or silver balls). Cut into shapes when almost cold.

COCONUT SWEETMEAT II
WITH FULL-CREAM POWDERED MILK

½ *teacupful* (1½ *oz.*) *fine desiccated coconut*	½ *pint ordinary milk*
5 *oz. sugar*	2 *oz. full-cream powdered milk*
1 *teaspoonful crushed cardamom seeds or grated nutmeg*	1 *dessertspoonful crushed walnuts or sliced coconut*

FOR 16 TO 18 SQUARES. Put the milk and coconut in a heavy aluminium frying pan, and boil fairly quickly until all the superfluous milk has dried out. Prepare the mock khoya by the usual method (see page 20), and put it in the frying mixture, mix and fry for another five minutes. Then add sugar, stir well and fry on medium heat until the mixture is fairly

dry—this should not take more than 10 minutes. Transfer to a shallow, buttered dish, and decorate with nuts and cardamom seeds.

Cut into pieces of the desired size when half-cold.

BARPHI I WITH CONDENSED MILK

4 oz. khoya (home-made condensed milk out of 1½ pints)

4 oz. sugar

1 teaspoonful cardamom seeds

1 dozen pistachio nuts (finely sliced)

1 tablespoonful ground almonds (optional)

Some silver leaf for decorating

FOR 12 PIECES. Make the khoya by boiling 1½ pints fresh milk until it is very thick. If you use a heavy aluminium frying pan, the condensing should not take more than an hour. Put aside and allow to cool. Then place khoya and sugar in a heavy aluminium saucepan, mix and cook very gently for nearly 10 minutes, taking care not to let the mixture stick to the bottom. Mix in ground almonds, and transfer mixture to a shallow dish that has been well greased with butter-fat. When slightly cool, pat and spread with the palm of the hand, and decorate with the crushed cardamom seeds and pistachio nuts and silver leaf. Cut slantwise into diamond shapes.

BARPHI II WITH FULL-CREAM POWDERED MILK

4 oz. full-cream powdered milk

8 oz. sugar

1 teacupful water

1 teaspoonful crushed cardamom seeds

1 dozen pistachio nuts (finely sliced)

Edible silver leaf or balls

FOR 20 PIECES. Boil the sugar and water fairly quickly for six or seven minutes. The syrup should then be so thick that a little of it dropped on a plate forms a round ball. Then add the powdered milk; mix well, and then turn the mixture onto a well-greased shallow plate. Pat and spread with the palm of your hand, and cut the mixture slantwise into diamond shapes.

Decorate with crushed cardamom seeds, pistachio nuts and the silver leaf or balls.

PERHAS

SWEETMEAT WITH CONDENSED MILK

4 oz. khoya (home-made condensed milk from 1½ pints milk)

4 oz. sugar (preferably caster)

1 teaspoonful set butter-fat

1½ dozen pistachio nuts

1 teaspoonful crushed cardamom seeds or grated nutmeg

FOR 10 PERHAS. Make the khoya by boiling 1½ pints of milk in a heavy aluminium frying pan, and allowing to cool. Warm the butter-fat in a heavy aluminium saucepan on a low heat.

Rub the khoya in your hands and break up any lumps, and put into the saucepan. Stir and mix for 4 to 5 minutes, still keeping on very low heat. Add sugar, and mix again for three minutes. When the sugar is warmed through and well mixed, remove the mixture from heat, and beat with a spoon for several minutes. When it is smooth and pliable, take a small portion, and, using the palm of your hand, shape it into a round biscuit (not too thin). Make each one separately, and place on a shallow dish that has been well greased with butter-fat. Decorate them with the finely sliced pistachio nuts and crushed cardamom seeds or grated nutmeg. When shaping the perhas, if the mixture is slightly sticky, it is permissible to use a little more of the caster sugar as you go along, but the mixture should not be allowed to get 'loose'.

BĀLU SHĀI

SUGAR-COATED SWEETMEAT

½ *lb. plain flour*
  (not wholemeal)
3 *oz. set butter-fat*
1½ *tablespoonfuls milk-curd*
  or warm milk

1 *teaspoonful baking powder*
½ *lb. fat for frying*
1 *tablespoonful warm water*

For syrup

10 *oz. sugar*

1½ *teacupfuls water*

FOR 18 BĀLU SHĀIS. Sieve the flour in a mixing bowl, add the well-heated butter-fat and the baking powder. Rub the mixture with your hands, gradually adding the milk-curd and warm water, and mix into a stiff dough. Break off a small portion of the dough, roll into a ball, then flatten it so that it resembles a small, round thick shortbread, and make a deep dent in the centre. Shape all the bālu shāis by this method.

To prepare the syrup, boil the sugar and water together in a large saucepan fairly quickly for seven to ten minutes: the syrup should be quite sticky. Keep this warm on a very low heat. Heat the frying fat in a chip pan, and fry the bālu shāis quite slowly until they are golden brown, and when they are done, put them in the warm syrup. When all are fried, let them simmer in the warm syrup for a few minutes, shaking the pan frequently to let them become well-coated with syrup. Take them out singly from the pan and place on a shallow dish. Serve cold at tea-time.

SHAKAR PĀRE

SUGAR-COATED CUBES

1 *teacupful plain flour*	1 *dessertspoonful ground*
(not wholemeal)	*almonds*
1 *tablespoonful set butter-fat*	*Some oil or fat for frying*
1-1½ *tablespoonfuls milk-curd*	
or milk	

For syrup

1 *teacupful sugar*	1 *teacupful water*

FOR 26 PIECES. Sieve the flour into a mixing bowl. Heat the butter-fat until smoking hot, and pour it onto the flour. Add the ground almonds, mix well, and gradually add heated-up milk-curd or milk. Knead this for several minutes, make the whole mixture into a smooth ball shape, then roll it out a little less than ½ inch thickness. Cut into inch long cubes. Heat the fat or oil in a deep chip pan, and bring carefully to nearly smoking point. Put in a handful of cubes at a time and fry very gently until the shakar pāre are of almond-skin colour. Drain, and put them straight into the syrup (which has been prepared beforehand by mixing the sugar and water together and boiling fairly quickly in a large saucepan for 7 to 8 minutes). When one lot has been dipped in the syrup, they should be taken out and placed on a shallow dish. When all are done, pour the remainder of the syrup over the lot, so that they get well-coated in sugar. When cold, they will be inclined to stick together a little, but they can easily be separated. Some of the dried sugar which remains at the bottom of the dish can be scraped off and put away for another use.

Shakar pāre are a traditional sweetmeat, and are served with other sweetmeats at marriage feasts.

STUFFED SWEET SAMOSAS

2 oz. plain flour
About 1 tablespoonful hot water
Some fat or oil for frying

½ oz. butter-fat
1 tablespoonful sliced pistachio nuts for decorating

For stuffing

2 oz. khoya (see page 20) or mock khoya
1 tablespoonful sultanas

½ teaspoonful crushed cardamom seeds
1 oz. sugar
1-2 dozen chopped almonds

For syrup

4 oz. sugar

½ teacupful water

FOR 8 SAMOSAS. Sieve the flour in a mixing bowl, add the ½ oz. of butter-fat, rubbing it in with your hands, and, by gradually adding the hot water, mix all into a stiff pastry.

To prepare the stuffing

Knead 2 oz. khoya (if mock khoya is being used, it should be prepared in advance by mixing 1½ tablespoonfuls water in 2 oz. dried milk). Add well washed, soaked and drained sultanas, chopped or ground nuts, 1 oz. sugar and the cardamom seeds, and mix well.

To make the syrup

Boil the 4 oz. sugar and ½ teacupful of water together fairly quickly for 3 to 4 minutes. The syrup should be quite sticky, but not stiff. Keep it slightly warm.

6

To shape samosas

Take a small portion of the pastry, shape into a ball, roll it out
with the help of a little dry flour as thin and round as possible.
Cut this pancake in half, take one semi-circle piece in your
hand, place 1 tablespoonful of stuffing on one half of this piece,
leaving the edges free, which should then be wetted with warm
water or milk. Now fold over the unfilled half on top of the
other and tightly close the edges together forming a three-
cornered stuffed cushion shape. Continue the process until all
the samosas are ready.

To fry the samosas

Heat the fat or oil in a chip pan, and fry the samosas singly and
quite slowly. After frying, dip each one in syrup, and place on
a shallow dish. The tops of the samosas can be decorated with
the sliced pistachio nuts. Some of the oil and syrup will be left
over, and can be used again.

The stuffing for the sweet samosas can be made out of
2 oz. of ground almonds instead of khoya or mock khoya.
The ground almonds should be mixed in a little cream, then
sugar, sultanas and crushed cardamom seeds or grated nutmeg
added to them.

Tea-Time Savouries

Tea-Time Savouries

MATTHIES

SAVOURY CAKES

3 teacupfuls (12 oz.) plain flour (not wholemeal)	1½ to 2 teaspoonfuls salt
2½ tablespoonfuls (4 oz.) set butter-fat	2 tablespoonfuls milk-curd or milk
1 dessertspoonful caraway seeds (optional)	2 tablespoonfuls (about) hot water
	1 pint liquid fat or frying oil

FOR 27 MATTHIES. Sieve the flour into a mixing bowl; heat the butter-fat to nearly smoking point and pour onto the flour. Add salt and caraway seeds, and mix it well with your hands, gradually adding the hot water and curd. The pastry for matthies should be quite stiff, and well worked. Take a small piece of pastry, and after making a ball of it, roll it out into the shape of a large, round biscuit (not too thin). Due to the stiffness of the pastry, the edges will be uneven.

Put the oil or fat in a deep frying pan, and bring it to nearly smoking point. Fry the matthies quite slowly, putting three or four in the pan at a time, turning with a slice whenever necessary. They should not be allowed to get really brown.

Small triangular-shaped or cube-shaped cakes can also be made. For the former, after shaping the piece of pastry into a ball, roll out into a small thin pancake, cut in half, and then fold twice into a triangular shape.

For a cube shape, roll a lump of pastry out in the same way as for biscuits, and cut into the desired shape.

Matthies are usually served cold, and are a great tea-time favourite. In an airtight tin, they will keep for nearly a fortnight.

PAKORHAS

SAVOURY VEGETABLE FRITTERS

For the batter

1½ teacupfuls besan (split-pea flour)	2 teaspoonfuls salt
	about 1 teacupful water
1 teaspoonful garam-masāla	½ teaspoonful turmeric
1 tablespoonful pomegranate seeds	½ teaspoonful chilli powder

For vegetables, etc.

1 large potato	1½ teaspoonfuls salt
1 large onion	½ teaspoonful garam-masāla
¼ lb. cauliflower	½ teaspoonful chilli powder
a few pieces of marrow or some spinach	about 1 pint oil or equivalent of fat for frying

To make the batter

FOR 20 TO 30 PAKORHAS. Sieve the flour in a mixing bowl, and gradually add the water. First make it as stiff as dough; then by continually adding a little more water, and beating hard all the time, bring it to the consistency of thick batter, and then leave for 30 minutes. Add salt, turmeric, garam-masāla, chilli powder and pomegranate seeds. Beat once again for several minutes, keeping the batter fairly thick.

To prepare the vegetables

Scrape, wash, and cut the potato into thin, round slices, and do the same with the onion. The pieces of cauliflower and marrow should be fairly thin and about 1½ inches long. Drain the vegetables well, mix salt, garam-masāla and chilli powder with them.

To fry the pakorhas

Using a deep frying pan, bring the oil or fat to nearly smoking point. Coat each piece of vegetable separately with the batter, and drop it into the hot fat. Fry as many pakorhas at a time as the pan will conveniently hold, on medium heat and not too quickly. Turn them frequently, and when golden brown all round, drain them well and remove from the pan.

Pakorhas are crisper if they are allowed to cool for a little while after frying, and then once again fried quickly before serving.

Besides the vegetables mentioned above, the following can also be used for pakorhas: Spinach, aubergines, green chillis, and capsicums (sweet peppers).

Some people mix vegetables, cut them small, wrap them in batter and fry them, instead of picking each one separately.

Potatoes can be boiled in their jackets, skinned and mashed well, and seasoned, and are then made into small flat cakes, coated well with the batter, and fried as ordinary pakorhas.

Pakorhas are a well-known Indian savoury delicacy, and are served hot or warm at tea-time with some mint or tamarind chutney.

SAMOSA ĀLŪ
TRIANGULAR CAKES, STUFFED WITH POTATO

For the stuffing

2 fairly large potatoes
1 small onion
2 tablespoonfuls broken-up dhania or other herbs
1 tablespoonful dried pomegranate seeds
A small piece of ginger, and ½ teaspoonful chilli powder (optional)

1½ teaspoonfuls salt
1 teaspoonful garam-masāla
1 dessertspoonful butter-fat
1 tablespoonful ground mango, or 1 dessertspoonful lemon juice

For pastry, etc.

1 teacupful plain flour (not wholemeal)
1 dessertspoonful butter-fat
Some oil or fat for frying

½ teaspoonful salt
2 tablespoonfuls, or more, milk-curd, or warm milk, for mixing

To prepare pastry for samosas

FOR 14 SAMOSAS. Sieve the flour in a mixing bowl, heat the butter-fat and pour it onto the flour. Add salt, and mix into a stiff pastry by gradually adding the milk-curd or warm milk.

For the stuffing

Boil the potatoes in their jackets: when cool, peel and mash them. Mince or finely chop the onion, herbs and ginger: heat the butter-fat in a frying pan, and fry the onion mixture in it very gently for two or three minutes. Add the prepared potatoes, the salt, garam-masāla, chilli powder, ground mango or lemon juice and the pomegranate seeds. Mix well, and keep on the heat for a short while until the mixture is well dry, then remove from heat, and keep by for stuffing the samosas.

To shape the samosas

Break off a little of the pastry, shape into a ball, roll it out with the help of a little dry flour as thin and round as possible. Cut this pancake in half, hold one semicircle in your hand, place about 1 tablespoonful of the potato mixture on one half of this piece, leaving the edges free, which should then be pasted inside and out with the milk-curd or milk. Now fold over the unfilled half on top of the other and tightly close the edges together.

Heat the fat or oil in a deep frying pan or chip pan. When smoking hot, fry the prepared samosas in it, two at a time, fairly slowly. When golden brown on both sides, drain well and remove from pan.

Samosas are usually served hot, with mint or tamarind chutney, at tea-time.

They are a great favourite with grown-ups and children alike.

SAMOSAS STUFFED WITH PEAS AND POTATO

For stuffing

3 *medium-sized potatoes*	2 *small tomatoes*
1 *teacupful freshly shelled peas*	1 *medium-sized onion*
	A small piece of ginger
1 *dessertspoonful set butter-fat*	1 *teaspoonful salt*
	1 *teaspoonful garam-masāla*
¼ *oz. dhania, or other herbs*	1 *dessertspoonful ground mango or lemon juice*
½ *teaspoonful (or more) chilli powder (optional)*	

For pastry, etc.

1 teacupful plain flour
(*not wholemeal*)
1 dessertspoonful set butter-
fat
Some oil or fat for frying

½ teaspoonful salt
2 tablespoonfuls (*or a little
more*) milk-curd or warm
milk for mixing

To prepare the stuffing

FOR 14 SAMOSAS. Boil potatoes in their jackets. When tender, let cool, skin them and cut into very small cubes (dicing). Using a deep frying pan, fry in the butter-fat the minced onions, ginger (if root ginger is used it should be soaked first) and the herbs. Add salt, chilli powder and sliced tomatoes. Stir well and allow to sizzle for a few minutes. Put in the peas, mix and cook gently (covered) for ten minutes. Next, mix in the diced potatoes, add garam-masāla and lemon juice, and cook till fairly dry before removing from heat.

Prepare the pastry as in previous recipe (page 168) and shape, stuff and fry the samosas as before. The peas and potatoes stuffing is inclined to open the edges of the samosas, so the inside and outside edges of each samosa should be slightly pasted with milk-curd before sticking together and frying.

SAMOSA STUFFED WITH MEAT

For stuffing

6 oz. lean minced meat
1 medium-sized onion
1 large tomato
1 large sweet pepper, or
¼ oz. fresh herbs
A small piece of ginger, and
½ teaspoonful chilli powder
(optional)
1 dessertspoonful butter-fat

½ teaspoonful turmeric
½ to 1 teaspoonful garam-masāla
1 teaspoonful salt
1 teacupful hot water
1 tablespoonful ground mango, or 1 dessertspoonful lemon juice

For pastry

1 teacupful plain flour
(not wholemeal)
1 dessertspoonful set butter-fat

½ teaspoonful salt
2 tablespoonfuls milk-curd or warm milk for mixing
Some oil or fat for frying

FOR 14 SAMOSAS. Prepare the pastry in the same manner as for other samosas.

For the stuffing—gently fry the minced onions, ginger and herbs together in the hot butter-fat. Add turmeric, salt and chilli powder. Fry for 2-3 minutes, then add the sliced tomatoes. Mix well, then put in the minced meat. Let it sizzle for five minutes, then pour the hot water on it. Bring to boil, then turn the heat very low, and cook for about 45 minutes. Add garam-masāla and the ground mango or lemon juice. Slightly mash the meat which should now be well cooked and dry. Allow to cool. Then stuff the samosas with the meat in the usual way. Paste the edges of samosas (inside and out) with the milk-curd or warm milk, close them properly, and fry in the hot fat, as before.

NAMKĪN BOONDI

SAVOURY DROPS

2 teacupfuls besan (split-pea flour)
½ teacupful (or little more) warm water
½ teaspoonful chilli powder (optional)
Some oil or fat for frying

½ teaspoonful garam-masāla
½ teaspoonful turmeric
1 tablespoonful butter-fat
1½ teaspoonfuls salt
½ to 1 teaspoonful ajowan seeds (optional)

2 slices or turners with medium-sized holes will be needed.

FOR 6 OR 7 PEOPLE. Sieve the flour into a mixing bowl, add salt, garam-masāla, and chilli powder. Heat the tablespoonful of butter-fat to boiling point, pour it on the flour, and mix well. Add the warm water gradually (split-pea flour will need a little more water), beating the mixture thoroughly as if making a sponge mixture: the more beating, the crisper the boondi will be. The texture should be like a thin, smooth cake mixture rather than batter. Heat the frying oil or fat in a large, deep frying pan or chip pan: place a large spoonful of the mixture onto a large, round slice or turner with medium-sized holes. With the laden slice in your right hand, and firmly gripping the handle of the frying pan with the other, tap the slice against the inner edges of the pan so that the boondi mixture falls into the smoking fat in droplets: not too much of the mixture at a time. Some of the boondi may be inclined to stick together, but they can easily be separated with the fingers after they have been fried. Frying should be done on a medium heat, and boondi should be golden brown all over, and well drained before being taken out of the pan. Repeat the process until all the mixture has been used. Remove the boondi onto another large shallow dish so that no superfluous fat is left on them.

When thoroughly cold, they should be kept in a tin. Namkīn boondi is usually served cold at tea-time, and is a great favourite.

SAVOURY SAVIA (SEV)

2 teacupfuls besan, or very fine split-pea flour
¼ teaspoonful turmeric
1 teaspoonful chilli powder (optional)
1½ tablespoonfuls (2 oz.) set butter-fat

2 teaspoonfuls salt
1 teaspoonful ajowan seeds, or any other savoury flavouring
About ½ teacupful warm water for mixing
Some oil or fat for frying

Sieve the flour into a mixing bowl: add salt and the rest of the ingredients, followed by the heated-up butter-fat. Rub well with your hands, and make it into a stiff dough by gradually adding the warm water. Knead for a few minutes.

Heat the deep fat or oil in a chip pan, place the dough in a clean 'Mouli-Shredder' with the finest gauge fixed, and pass the dough through to form thin strips. In India we use a machine similar to that used to make vermicelli or the small macaroni. This is held over the pan, and the strips drop straight into the hot fat. Fry these slowly in the near-smoking fat, repeating the process until all the dough is used up.

Savoury savia are very tasty, crisp and crunchy, and are served at tea-time.

ĀLŪ TIKIA
SIMILAR TO POTATO RISSOLES

1 lb. potatoes
1 teaspoonful set butter-fat
1 teaspoonful garam-masāla
4 spring onions
1 egg
1 dessertspoonful lemon juice
some oil or fat for frying
1½ teaspoonfuls salt

1 teacupful freshly shelled peas
1 to 2 tablespoonfuls broken-up dhania or other fresh herbs
¼ oz. finely chopped ginger, and ½ teaspoonful chilli powder, or 2 chopped fresh green chillies (optional)

FOR 12 TIKIA. Prepare the potato pastry by the same method as given for potato koftas (see page 83); and beat the egg.

Heat the butter-fat in a small saucepan: wash the peas and put them in the saucepan. Sprinkle a little salt and water on them, cover, and allow to simmer until tender, which should not take more than 6 to 7 minutes. Remove from heat, and when slightly cold, crush them a little and mix them in the potato pastry. Add minced onion, ginger, herbs, the remainder of the salt, garam-masāla, chopped fresh chillies or chilli powder, and the lemon juice. Mix thoroughly, and shape the tikia like thin round rissoles. Fry them in shallow, hot fat on medium heat, after dipping them in the egg mixture.

Serve hot or cold at any meal with chutney.

ĀLŪ LACHCHE
SAVOURY POTATO STRAWS

2 medium-sized potatoes
1 teaspoonful salt
1 teaspoonful ground caraway seeds

1 dessertspoonful ground mango, and ½ teaspoonful chilli powder (optional)
Some oil or fat for frying

Scrape, wash, and grate the potatoes: place in a colander and wash them again under running water. Drain and dry them well in a teacloth. All this has to be done fairly quickly. Using a chip pan, bring the deep fat or oil to smoking point, and then fry the straws a handful at a time on medium heat.

When the straws are of a golden brown colour, take them out of the pan by means of a large slice with very small holes in it, and after draining off the fat, place them on a shallow dish.

When all are done, shift them onto another dish and mix in them the rest of the ingredients.

Ālū lachche are very tasty, and are usually served at tea-time.

NAMAK PĀRĒ

SAVOURY CUBES

1 *teacupful plain flour (not wholemeal)*
1 *tablespoonful set butter-fat*
¾ *teaspoonful salt*
Some oil or fat for frying

1 *to* 1½ *tablespoonfuls curd or water*
1 *teaspoonful caraway or ajowan seeds (optional)*

Sieve the flour into a mixing bowl. Heat the butter-fat to smoking point, and pour onto the flour. Add salt, and the ajowan or caraway seeds, mix well, and gradually add the heated curd or water. Knead for several minutes; shape the whole of the pastry into a ball, and roll out on a bread-board to about ½-inch thickness.

Cut into cubes of the desired size, and fry a handful at a time, quite slowly, until they are the colour of almond skin.

Namak pārē are served cold at tea-time, or with cold drinks.

CHANNA DĀL OR SPLIT PEAS (FRIED)

1 teacupful channa dāl   ½ teaspoonful garam-masāla
   (see page 22)   ¼ teaspoonful chilli powder and
1 tablespoonful bicarbonate   1 dessertspoonful ground
   soda   mango (optional)
1 teaspoonful salt   Some oil or fat for frying

Soak the split peas in plenty of water, to which the bicarbonate soda has been added. After soaking 18 hours, take them
out and soak them again for another 12 hours in fresh water.
Then drain well and spread out on a clean cloth to dry, for at
least an hour. Heat the oil or fat in a heavy chip pan on medium
heat, and when smoking hot fry a handful of split peas at a
time, keeping on medium heat all the while. When they float
on the top, allow a little more frying, and then take them out
with a large round slice which has small holes. Drain well, and
spread onto a shallow plate or tray.

When all the channa dāl is fried, place on a clean cloth and
wipe off as much of the oil as possible. When partially cool
coat them with the salt, garam-masāla, chilli powder and
ground mango mixed together.

Fried channa dāl is crisp and very tasty, and is usually
served at tea-time.

Dāl urhad (see page 22) can also be fried by the same
method, but reducing the soaking time to 18 hours.

NĀN-KHATĀI

SEMOLINA SHORTBREADS

6 oz. semolina   1 dozen or more pistachio
2 oz. plain or self-raising   kernels or almond nuts
   flour (not wholemeal)   1 teaspoonful crushed
4 oz. set butter-fat   cardamom seeds, or grated
4 oz. sugar   nutmeg

FOR 22 SHORTBREADS. Beat the butter-fat and sugar together for several minutes, until the mixture is almost like cream. Gradually add the already sieved semolina and flour. Mix and beat once again, add crushed cardamom seeds or nutmeg. No liquid is needed.

Leave the mixture for 30 minutes or so: then knead well with your hands until it is very smooth to handle. Take a little of it, shape into a small round shortcake, and place it on a well-greased tin: then repeat until all the nān-khatāis are prepared. Decorate them with finely sliced kernels or nuts, and bake them in the oven on Regulo 5 or 6 until they are a nice almond colour, which should take about half an hour.

When thoroughly cold, keep in a tin.

SŪJI KARKARIAS
SEMOLINA FRIED CAKES

1 tablespoonful set butter-fat
5 oz. sugar
1 pint milk
4 oz. semolina
2 eggs
½ lb. of fat, for frying

1 teaspoonful crushed cardamoms or nutmeg, or other sweet flavouring
1 tablespoonful ground almonds

FOR 16 SMALL CAKES. Using an aluminium saucepan, mix the semolina in a little milk, then gradually add the rest of the milk. After adding the butter-fat and sugar, boil this mixture slowly until it is fairly thick, stirring all the time. Remove from heat and allow to cool.

Beat the eggs, and mix in the cold semolina mixture. Add crushed cardamoms or grated nutmeg, and mix thoroughly.

Heat the fat in a deep chip pan to nearly smoking point. Take a dessertspoonful of the mixture, and fry it in the fat:

several spoonfuls can be fried at a time. When golden brown both sides, drain and remove from the pan. Repeat the process until all the mixture is finished.

These cakes are crunchy and tasty; and are served cold at tea-time.

GOL GAPPAS

(These are small, round, hollow wafers, filled with savoury juice, or other stuffing)

For wafers

1 teacupful plain flour (not wholemeal)	½ teaspoonful, or less, of salt
½ teacupful warm water	Some oil or fat for frying

For savoury juice

1 pint of water	1-2 teaspoonfuls caraway seeds
2 oz. tamarind or ground mango, or 2 tablespoonfuls lemon juice	½ teaspoonful garam-masāla
2 tablespoonfuls chopped mint	1 teaspoonful salt
½ teaspoonful chilli powder (optional)	A pinch of ground ginger

To make savoury juice

FOR 40 WAFERS. Rinse and soak the tamarinds in half the water for 15 minutes, then rub the fruit with your fingers so that all the pulp comes away from the stones. Add the rest of the water, mix and strain through a strainer (not too fine), and throw away the stones and fibres. Add the rest of the ingredients, all finely ground and chopped, to this tamarind juice: mix well and leave for two hours. To save time, the savoury juice may be prepared by just mixing all the ingredients and boiling them for 5 to 7 minutes, then letting the juice get thoroughly cold before serving.

To make gol gappas

Sieve the flour in a mixing bowl, add salt, and first make it into a very stiff pastry by adding as little water as possible. Knead hard for several minutes, and keep adding a little more water until you have used up about ½ teacupful. Knead once again, then taking some of this pastry, make it into a round ball, and with the help of a little dry flour, roll it out as thin as you can. Cut out quite small, round biscuit-shaped pieces, and fry them in deep fat on medium heat, two or three at a time. They should rise like balloons. Continue turning them, and when they are well cooked and brown, drain them and place on a shallow dish.

Gol gappas are served cold, and are eaten filled with the savoury juice, which is put in after making a hole in the centre of each gol gappa.

They may also be eaten filled with cooked kabli channas (page 108); potato chāt (below); or dahi pakori (page 134).

ALU CHĀT
POTATO DISCS

1 lb. potatoes (*preferably small*)
1½ teaspoonfuls salt
½ teaspoonful ground caraway seeds

2 tablespoonfuls lemon juice
2 small chopped green chillies, or ½ teaspoonful chilli powder (*optional*)
½ teaspoonful garam-masāla

Scrub and boil the potatoes in their jackets. When cool, peel and slice them into small, round pieces. Place on a shallow dish, and mix the rest of the ingredients in them.

Ālū chāt is very tasty served in salad.

Instead of lemon juice, the pulp of 1½ oz. of tamarinds can be used, which can be prepared by soaking the tamarinds in half a cupful of water, and working the pulp away from the stones with your fingers.

Sweet potato chāt and *mixed fruit chāt* can be prepared the same way.

The fruits, such as bananas, apples, pears, plums, etc., are just cut into small pieces, mixed together, and then the salt, garam-masāla, ground caraway seeds, chopped green chillies or chilli powder mixed in with them.

Chāts are usually eaten with small sticks, similar to the ones used in picking cherries out of cocktails.

Pickles and Chutneys

Pickles and Chutneys

LIME OR LEMON PICKLE I (IN OIL)

2 lb. green or slightly yellow
  limes or lemons
3 tablespoonfuls salt
1 teaspoonful turmeric
1 tablespoonful somph
  (aniseed)
1½ teaspoonfuls crushed
  mustard seeds

1-2 teaspoonfuls garam-
  masāla
1-2 teaspoonfuls chilli powder
A few green or red chillies
  (optional)
¼ pint mustard oil

Cut the limes or lemons into squares; remove all pips, taking
care to catch the juice in a jug. If small limes are used, they
need not be cut right through. Heat one tablespoonful mustard
oil in a saucepan; add turmeric, salt, and the rest of the
ingredients. Mix and simmer for a minute or two, then remove
from heat. Mix or stuff the fruit with this oily mixture; shake
well, and shift the pickle into a jar. Cover well, and keep in a
warm cupboard for a week or a fortnight, shaking it every day,
and putting it out in the sun whenever possible. After that, add
the rest of the oil so that the pickle is well saturated with it.
More oil can be used if necessary; but only mustard oil is suitable for this pickle.

In India, unripe green mangoes, whole green chillies, young
bamboo-shoots, jack fruit, fresh ginger, and a variety of other
fruits and vegetables are pickled by the above method.

NOTE: Mustard oil can be obtained from your local chemist
and from the Indian grocers.

183

LIME OR LEMON PICKLE II
(WITHOUT OIL)

2 *lb. limes or lemons*
3-4 *tablespoonfuls salt*
1 *teaspoonful turmeric*

2 *teaspoonfuls garam-masāla*
1-2 *teaspoonfuls chilli powder*
A few green chillies (optional)

Cut the limes or lemons into pieces of the desired size, and remove all pips, as given in the previous recipe. Mix in salt, turmeric, chilli powder and garam-masāla. Green chillies should be washed and drained before mixing in the pickle. Turn into a screw-topped jar, and keep the pickle in a warm cupboard, or if possible, in the hot sun for a week, giving it a good shaking every day. When the skins are tender, then the pickle will be ready. Store it, well covered, and shake it now and then.

This pickle is especially nice with fish preparations.

LIME OR LEMON PICKLE III
(SWEET PICKLE)

1½ *lb. limes or lemons*
1½ *teaspoonfuls salt*
½ *teaspoonful turmeric*

1-2 *teaspoonfuls garam-masāla*
1-2 *teaspoonfuls chilli powder*
6 *oz. demerara sugar*

Cut the limes or lemons into pieces of the desired size; remove all pips, as usual. Mix in salt, turmeric, brown sugar, garam-masāla and the chilli powder; shake well, and after putting the lid on, keep in a warm cupboard, or in the sun for a week, as directed for the previous recipe.

This pickle will also be ready to eat when the skins of the lemons are reasonably tender. The addition of the sugar seems to give it an unusually piquant taste.

If well covered, and shaken now and then, this pickle should keep for several months.

GOOSEBERRY PICKLE

1 lb. firm gooseberries
1 tablespoonful salt
1 teaspoonful, or more aniseeds
1 dessertspoonful crushed black mustard seeds
1½ teaspoonfuls garam-masāla
4 tablespoonfuls or more mustard oil
1 teaspoonful turmeric
1-2 teaspoonfuls chilli powder (optional)

Top and tail the gooseberries, wash and drain them. Heat one tablespoon of the oil in a saucepan, and very gently fry in that the turmeric, salt and the rest of the ingredients excepting the gooseberries. Remove from heat then mix in the gooseberries. Transfer the pickle into a jar with a tight lid, and put it in a warm cupboard for a week, shaking it regularly and putting it out in the sun whenever possible. After that add the rest of the oil so that the pickle is well saturated in oil. Store in a cool place.

SWEET CAULIFLOWER PICKLE

2½ lb. cauliflower (in pieces)
½ bulb garlic
¾ oz. root ginger, fresh or dried
1 dessertspoonful chilli powder
2-3 tablespoonfuls salt
1 dessertspoonful turmeric
2 tablespoonfuls mustard oil
½ lb. brown sugar
¼ pint malt vinegar
1 dessertspoonful crushed black mustard seeds
1 tablespoonful garam-masāla
2 oz. tamarind

The pieces of cauliflower should be of medium size; they should be brought to the boil just once, and allowed to cool. Mince garlic and ginger together, and fry these gently in the mustard oil until golden brown, mash well and keep by you. Mix the brown sugar and vinegar together and boil slowly until fairly thick. Remove from heat, and when thoroughly cold, mix in it the crushed mustard, salt, chilli powder, turmeric and garam-masāla. Add the fried garlic and ginger with the oil; mix well, and finally put in the pieces of cauliflower.

Soak the tamarind in a little water, then rub the pulp from the stones; strain through a coarse strainer, and add to the pickle. Shake and mix thoroughly, and shift into a large jar. Keep in a warm place for a week, giving it a good shaking every day. At the end of this time, it should be ready.

Carrots and turnips can be used instead of cauliflower. The rest of the ingredients and the method will be the same.

CAULIFLOWER PICKLE
(SWEET OR OTHERWISE)

2 lb. pieces of cauliflower
2 tablespoonfuls salt
1 tablespoonful crushed black mustard seeds
1 dessertspoonful turmeric

1 dessertspoonful garam-masāla
1 dessertspoonful chilli powder
¼ lb. ginger (fresh or dried)

Extra Ingredients

4-6 oz. brown sugar
2 oz. dried tamarind (not pulp)

3 tablespoonfuls vinegar
1 teacupful water for the tamarind

Break the cauliflower into 1½-2 inch long pieces (not too thin). Wash and bring them to boil just once; drain well and cool. Root ginger should be soaked in advance, then sliced. Place the pieces in a large glass jar; add salt, turmeric, chilli powder, black mustard seeds (crushed), garam-masāla and the sliced ginger. Shake vigorously, cover and keep it in a warm cupboard or in the sun for a few days.

After that, some people like to use the pickle as it is, but to make it more tasty and sweet, the second lot of ingredients are mixed in the following way: Soak the tamarind in one teacupful of water and get all the pulp out, and pour it on the pickle. Mix vinegar and brown sugar together, and boil for 2-3 minutes, then add that to the pickle, and shake well.

The pickle should be ready to use after a day or two.

Carrots, turnips and salad cabbage can be pickled by the above method. The cabbage should be shredded and pickled without boiling.

KANJI

CARROT PICKLE WITH JUICE

2½ lb. fresh carrots	4 tablespoonfuls mustard seeds
¼ lb. fresh beetroot	1 tablespoonful garam-masāla
4-6 tablespoonfuls cooking salt	1 dessertspoonful or more chilli powder
6-8 pints of water	

Scrape, wash, and cut the carrots and beetroot into thin round or two-inch-long pieces. Mix salt, crushed mustard seeds, garam-masāla and chilli powder. Shake well and then pour in the cold boiled water. Keep this in a warm place for a week. The pickle should be of pale pink colour when it is ready.

The juice is the essential part of this pickle. It should be poured out in small glasses, and served before or after the midday meal.

The beetroot is only added in this pickle for its colour, as a substitute for the maroon coloured carrots we get in India, and if more than the amount given in the recipe is used, it will spoil the taste of the pickle.

MIXED FRUIT CHUTNEY

½ lb. cooking apples	1-2 teaspoonfuls chilli powder
½ lb. cooking plums	1 teaspoonful caraway seeds
½ lb. cooking pears or	(optional)
apricots	12 cloves of garlic
2 tablespoonfuls sultanas	¼ oz. root ginger (fresh or
¾-1 lb. brown sugar	dried)
8 fluid oz. vinegar	1 dessertspoonful salt
1-2 teaspoonfuls garam-masāla	

TO MAKE 2 LBS. Wash, dry and stone the plums, and cut them in small pieces. Core and thinly peel the apples and pears, and cut them in small pieces also. If dry root ginger is being used, it should be soaked for a few hours in advance, then minced with the garlic. Place the cut fruit in a spacious enamel saucepan, add the rest of the ingredients, including the sugar and the vinegar. Boil on medium heat for nearly 40 minutes, stirring frequently with a wooden spoon and crushing the fruit slightly. Remove from heat, and allow to get thoroughly cold before bottling.

This chutney is very tasty, and has an attractive appearance.

GOOSEBERRY CHUTNEY

1½ lb. fresh, firm
    gooseberries
1 lb. sugar
1 dessertspoonful salt
12 cloves of garlic
1 teaspoonful caraway
    seeds (optional)

2 oz. sweet preserved ginger
    or ¼ oz. root ginger
1-2 teaspoonfuls chilli powder
1-2 teaspoonfuls garam-
    masāla
7 liquid oz. malt vinegar

ENOUGH ALMOST TO FILL A 2 LB. JAR. Wash and drain the
gooseberries, skin and mince finely the cloves of garlic and
ginger (if root ginger is used, it should be soaked for several
hours in advance). Put the gooseberries in a spacious enamel
saucepan, and add the sugar and the rest of the ingredients,
the vinegar last of all. Boil on a fairly low heat for 20-30
minutes, stirring frequently with a wooden spoon to prevent
sticking. The chutney should not be allowed to get really
thick before removing from heat, bearing in mind that when
it cools it will naturally thicken. Neither should the fruit be
crushed more than can be helped.

The chutney should be stored only when it is thoroughly
cold.

GREEN TOMATO CHUTNEY

2 lb. firm green tomatoes
1 tablespoon salt
1½ to 2 teaspoonfuls chilli
    powder
½ oz. root ginger (fresh or
    dry)

1 lb. sugar, preferably brown
1½-2 teaspoonfuls garam-
    masāla
15 cloves of garlic
12 liquid oz. malt vinegar
1½ teaspoonfuls caraway seeds
    (optional)

Rinse, dry and cut the tomatoes into small pieces; skin and mince the garlic and ginger. If dried root ginger is used, it should be soaked for a few hours in advance, and then minced. Place the tomatoes in a heavy enamelled saucepan, add sugar, vinegar, and the rest of the ingredients. Cook these on medium heat for 50 to 55 minutes, stirring frequently with a wooden spoon and crushing the tomatoes slightly after they have become soft. Remove from heat, and cool thoroughly before pouring into jars.

The chutney should be stored in a cool place.

BLACK OR RED CURRANT CHUTNEY

12 oz. firm red or
  blackcurrants

6 good eating dates (stoned
  and cut small)

Apart from the fact that black or red currants are substituted for the gooseberries, and the dates are added, the ingredients for this chutney are the same as for the Gooseberry Chutney (page 189). The method of preparation is the same, and the cooking time on medium heat is from 15 to 20 minutes.

PODINA CHUTNEY
MINT CHUTNEY

6 medium-sized spring onions
1 teacupful ready-to-use
  mint
1 teaspoonful salt
1 teaspoonful sugar
2 medium-sized minced green
  chillies or ½ teaspoonful
  chilli powder

½ teaspoonful garam-masāla
1 tablespoonful dried
  pomegranate seeds
1 dessertspoonful ground
  mango or 1 tablespoonful
  lemon juice

FOR 5 PEOPLE. Wash the onions, throwing away only the tough green leaves. Wash the mint under running water, and mince these two things and the fresh green chillies together. Put them in a mortar, add salt, sugar and garam-masāla and crush for several minutes with the pestle. Take out and place aside on a plate. Sort and rinse the dried pomegranate seeds, and crush them in the mortar separately, then put the half-prepared chutney back in the mortar and crush and mix thoroughly. Lastly add the ground mango or lemon juice and mix once again. Transfer to a glass dish and serve.

Mint chutney will keep for a day or two, but is tastier when freshly made.

NOTE: Dried pomegranate (anardāna) can be obtained from Indian grocers.

DHANIA CHUTNEY
CORIANDER CHUTNEY

The ingredients and method for this are the same as those for mint chutney, except that coriander is substituted for mint, and pomegranate seeds are omitted.

IMALI CHUTNEY
TAMARIND CHUTNEY

4 oz. of good dried tamarind	1 teaspoonful salt
about a teacupful of water	1 teaspoonful garam-masāla
1 tablespoonful sugar	½ teaspoonful chilli powder

Rinse and soak the tamarind in some of the water for a few minutes, then rub it well with your fingers, to separate the pulp from the stones and fibre. Gradually add the rest of the water. Put this mixture in a strainer with medium-sized holes, placing a small bowl underneath. Press the mixture through the strainer with a wooden spoon, so that all the pulp comes out from it. The dry fibre and stones should be thrown away. The pulp will be fairly thick and will contain small bits of tamarind which are quite harmless. Add the rest of the ingredients to the pulp. Mix thoroughly and the chutney will be ready.

This chutney will keep only for a day or two, and is served with many Indian savoury delicacies.